SILENCE

Surviving IN SILENCE

OVERCOMING DOMESTIC VIOLENCE

A COMPILATION OF WOMEN OVERCOMING AND SURVIVING ON PURPOSE!

CHEMEKA TURNER-WILLIAMS

Surviving In Silence

Printed in the United States of America

ISBN-13: 978-0-9998789-2-7
Library of Congress Cataloging-in-Publication Data

Domestic Violence Resources:
National Coalition Against Domestic Violence (NCADV) & As Referenced.

Book Coaching & Editing by:
SynergyEd Consulting/ www.synergyedconsulting.com

Cover Design: Orin Perry- D&K Productions
Graphics & Marketing: Greenlight Creations- glightcreations.com
Photography: Lakisha Newell/ Her Camera Photography- hercamera83@gmail.com

Published by: SHERO PUBLISHING
SHEROPublishing.com
For copies and publishing information, email: ericaperrygreen@gmail.com

Table of Contents

Overcomers!

Dedication

This book is dedicated to all the women and children all over the world who have suffered at the hands of domestic violence and abuse, and those who tragically lost their lives to this increasing epidemic. I'm applauding, honoring, and uplifting all the women, and children who are gaining the boldness, bravery, and the courage to stand up and speak out in their situation. Understanding that it's not easy, and that it takes strength to OVERCOME such great, and traumatic experiences.

God Bless You,

Chemeka Turner- Williams

Acknowledgements

I am grateful to those who supported and encouraged me as I worked on this God given assignment.

Giving honor to my Lord and Savior Jesus Christ. Without Him, nothing would be possible! He is my Light and my strength and without him, I would still be in darkness. He has kept me and protected me. I am thankful for His hand, that is on my life. I thank Him for trusting me to fulfill this assignment.

To my children Tatiyanna, Shaleik, Nacyiah, Naseyah, I love you beyond words!!! You have been with me every step of the way cheering me on. Thank you for your continuous encouragement and believing in mommy's vision. Each of you gave me hope to hold on to, when it seemed as if there was none left. You spoke Gods' word over me when doubt tried to creep in. You prayed for me when I didn't have the strength to pray for myself. And for that, I'm grateful. I persevere and endure daily to show you that all things are possible through Christ Jesus and to leave an inheritance and a legacy through each of you. Keep God first in EVERYTHING!! I love each of you!!

To My mother, Angela Faye Turner, thank you for your prayers and for pushing me when I needed it the most. Thank you for your sacrifices and raising me to be the woman I am today. Your strength to overcome speaks volumes. You have been a great example to each of us. You are and always will be my SUPERWOMAN. Your legacy lives on through me.

To My Pastor and Spiritual Father, Orin Perry, thank you for keeping me lifted-up in the kingdom of God. Thank you for pouring out your spiritual wisdom, your guidance, your sound biblical teachings and all of your sacrifices over the years. Thank you for being there to intercede for me and lead me to God when I was searching for a path. You graced me with so much favor and success. I thank you for seeing the best in me and giving me the opportunity to grow. Thank you for showing me another level of excellence and servitude.

To my spiritual mother, Mary Perry Howell, your prayers did not go unfulfilled. Your constant wisdom and motivation shaped and molded me, in preparation for the next chapter of my life. Thank you for your guidance and walking me through my healing process. You taught me how to suffer with class, while holding on to the promises of God.

To my siblings: Derrick, Angela, Tishena, and Trevor, thank you for your encouragement and motivation. I LOVE YOU!

I pray this book is a blessing to you all!

You are more than a survivor; you are an OVERCOMER!!

Introduction

Domestic violence is the most common form of violence against women and is evident, to some degree, in every society in the world. The World Health Organization reports that the proportion of women who have ever experienced physical or sexual violence or both by an intimate partner ranges from 15% to 71%, with the majority between 29% and 62%. (1)

"Domestic violence is a burden on numerous sectors of the social system and quietly, yet dramatically, affects the development of a nation... batterers cost nations fortunes in terms of law enforcement, health care, lost labor and general progress in development. These costs do not only affect the present generation; what begins as an assault by one person on another, reverberates through the family and the community into the future". (2) Domestic violence and abuse is a global epidemic reaching across national boundaries as well as socio-economic, racial, cultural, and class distinctions. This epidemic is not only increasing geographically, but its incidence is also extensive, making it a normal and accepted behavior by our societies. Domestic violence is widespread, deeply knitted in our communities and cultures and has serious impacts on women's health and well-being. The national economic cost of domestic and family violence and abuse is estimated to be over 12 billion dollars per year. According to the World Health Organization the numbers of individuals affected is expected to rise over the next 20 years with the increase in the elderly population.

Even with reports of these alarming figures, they are likely to be significantly underestimated due to the fact that violence within families continues to be a taboo and hush subject in our cultures and societies. This pervasive issue has been overlooked, ignored, and stitched in the fabric of our society as normality. "Domestic violence is not simply an argument. It is a pattern of coercive control that one person exercises over another. Abusers use physical and sexual violence, threats, emotional insults and economic deprivation as a way to dominate their victims and get their way". (Susan Scheter, visionary leader in the movement to end family violence)

What Is Domestic Abuse?

The term domestic abuse, also called intimate partner violence (IPV), has been identified as the systematic suffocation of another person's spirit. It's ultimately about power and control. There's an unbalance and one person holds ALL the power and therefore uses it to control the other person; the victim. Domestic abuse includes, but is not limited to physical, emotional, spiritual, economic and sexual abuse.

Quite often when we think of domestic abuse or try to identify with it, the first thing we usually visualize is hitting, choking, slapping, punching, kicking, physical attacks.

Abuse is so much more than the physical attributes. It also includes having someone do the following:

- Call you names
- Constantly criticize
- Constantly make jokes about your appearance
- Consistently ignore your feelings
- Throw items at you
- Humiliate you in front of others
- Belittle your accomplishments
- Insist on making decisions for you
- Insist you have an *issue* or you are crazy
- Prevent you from practicing your faith
- Judge you harshly
- Force you to have sex
- Make demeaning comments about your gender
- Withhold affection

Research has shown that while there are several behaviors that are similar in almost all abusive relationships, there are as many variations on the style and severity of abuse as there are perpetrators. (1.) One might easily think that abuse is about anger that is out of control. That is only a fraction of the issue. Anger is only one of the many tools and tactics used by an abuser to establish fear in the victim; to dominate and make her compliant. Abuse is a choice. Anyone who can choose to hit can choose not to hit. It's a choice; it's a decision. You aren't responsible for the abuser's choice. You don't deserve any kind of abuse under any circumstance or for any reason. Remember YOU CAN NOT make the abuser change.

Some people think a mental health disorder/disease or problems with alcohol or other drug use causes abuse. Although mental health disorders may be a factor in some cases, most research shows a low rate of mental health disorder in even the most violent abusers. Alcohol and drugs only serve to make it easier for the abuser to act on his impulses, heighten and intensify the behavior and the root cause of the issue.

Physical violence is easier to identify as abuse because it leaves bruises and marks on the body that are visible. We can easily see the black eyes, busted lips, scratches, broken bones, stitches, blood and bandages. But what about those INVISIBLE SCARS of emotional, mental, spiritual, economic and sexual abuse that are just as destructive and life threatening. What about those hidden scars that we try to cover up and mask with a SMILE? No matter the type of abuse, it will leave emotional scars and imprint on your spirit. A broken leg, arm, or cheekbone can heal in a matter of weeks. BUT a wounded *Spirit* can last a lifetime and affect every aspect of your life UNTIL *you* LET THE HEALING BEGIN.

Who Is a Victim?

Domestic violence is a general term that refers to any abuse that occurs within a familiar type relationship; victims include romantic partners, children, or elderly people. In romantic relationships, the partners may be married, living together, or dating. Both heterosexual and homosexual relationships can become abusive, and abusers can be either male or female. In this book we will focus on the women who have been the victims.

Domestic violence and abuse can be experienced by women from their early teen years through later life. There is no set age. Statistics show that about one in three high school girls date a boy who slaps, punches, strangles, shoves, or kicks her. Statistics show that females who are twenty to twenty-four years old are at the greatest risk for nonfatal intimate partner violence. (3)

Abuse is subtle. It escalates so slowly that you may not realize where it's taking you or that it is happening to you. Abuse may start off with a derogatory comment here and there. Then it may be insulting jokes and laughs directed towards you, then it is a strong hold on your arm or aggressive grabbing. If you confront him, he tells you it's no big deal, he's just playing, or he didn't mean to do it. He convinces you that you are overreacting, you are too sensitive, you are too emotional, or that's just the way he is. As the abuse grows, he manipulates you to believe he's the one in pain and he needs you. He guilts you into accepting these negative behaviors and then you ignore the red flags in front of you. You believe him and are sure that if you can just love him enough, he will change. Because you care about him, you adjust your thinking to allow yourself to stay in this impossible situation.

Research shows that long-term exposure to emotional abuse causes chemical changes in the brain. As a result, the victim's view of the severity of the abuse becomes distorted. You now begin to accept and believe that what you are experiencing is normal and it's nothing wrong with these behaviors. Many forms of verbal and psychological abuse appear relatively harmless at first, but these incidents expand and grow more violent over time, sometimes gradually and subtly. As victims adapt to abusive behavior, the verbal or psychological tactics can gain a strong 'foothold' in victims' minds, making it difficult for them to recognize the severity of the abuse over time. You will notice and find that most victims minimize or downplay the abusers actions. The victim even begins to make excuses and cover for the abuser.

If you are thinking the way I use to think, you are holding on to the fantasy or hope that one day he will wake up sorry for all he has put you through; that he will become the man that he has the potential to be,or he will see the value in you as a woman. . As long as he refuses to admit what he is doing, and will not get help to stop this behavior, the abuse will continue and its severity will escalate. This will be the start of the domestic violence cycle.

The TRUTH is if he hits you once, he will SURELY hit you again and again and again. If he humiliates you once, know that he will do it again with no remorse. People with abusive behavior and tendencies do what works for them and what they can get away with. If controlling you through bullying, manipulation, charisma, threats, or physical attacks gets him what he wants, why would he desire to change or attempt to change?

According to the World Health Organization, over both the short term and long term, women's physical injuries and mental distress either interrupts, or ends, their educational and career paths, thus leading to poverty and economic dependence. Family life gets disrupted, which has a significant effect on children, including poverty (if divorce or separation occurs) and a loss of faith and trust in the institution of the family. (4)

WE ARE IN A STATE OF EMERGENCY!!! A CODE RED has been declared to help those women and children impacted by domestic violence and abuse. Sound the alarm!!! NO MORE SILENCE!!! NO MORE COVERING UP THIS ISSUE!!! NO MORE SHAME AND GUILT!!! YOUR VOICE MATTERS!!! SURVIVING IN SILENCE: OVERCOMING DOMESTIC VIOLENCE tells the POWERFUL stories of ten courageous women who survived and overcame domestic violence and abuse. Each was a victim of domestic violence, but survived to tell the story and educate and bring awareness to this global epidemic that has gone hidden and covered up for too long. Every woman who has ever experienced abuse or is experiencing abuse will find encouragement, hope, and renewed strength in the voices of these women who broke free.

This book will provide a pathway for victims of abuse to become true SURVIVORS and OVERCOMERS. This book will be an excellent resource for families, friends, ministries, churches, and community outreach programs who desire to provide support to those impacted by domestic violence. Important information, skills, steps, and strategies are explained to help guide one through the experience and the healing process.NO MORE SILENCE!! Women are using their voices to take back their lives, reclaim their dignity, build on a new foundation and discover that there is life after abuse. There is PURPOSE within the OVERCOMER!

1. World Health Organizationa (WHO) Multi country study on Women's health and domestic violence against women. Geneva: World Health Organization; 2007. [Google Scholar]
2. Zimmerman C. Plates in a basket will rattle: Domestic violence in Combodia, Phnom Pehn. Combodia: The Asia Foundation; 1994. [Google Scholar]
3. Intimate Partner Violence in the U.S.," U.S. Department of Justice, Bureau of Justice Statistics, December 2006,
4. www.ojp.usdoj.gov/bjs/intimate/victims.htm
5. World Health Organization (WHO).Domestic violence: A priority public health issue in western Pacific region. Western Pacific Regional Office. 2001 [Google Scholar]

Thank You Authors

I thank God for the BIRTHING of **Surviving in Silence: Overcoming Domestic Violence**! I am grateful for each OVERCOMER that is a part of this collaboration project. I am thankful that you decided to share your stories with the world so that everyone can see that there is life after abuse. Each of you are extraordinary and you give hope to the hopeless, and strength to the weak. You let women who are suffering know there is a way out.

To each of you BOLD and BEAUTIFUL ladies, I say, THANK YOU! THANK YOU for entrusting me with your very personal and powerful testimonies. Thank you for sharing how you made it over, in this life changing literary work. ~ Chemeka Turner Williams, Visionary

Author

Chemeka Turner Williams

Chemeka Turner Williams

Chemeka Turner-Williams is a woman of "many hats". She's been described as a "new and unique voice in the earth"; delivering entrenched messages of inspiration and empowerment from a fresh perspective. Chemeka has harvested foundations of skilled advocacy, oratorical abilities and scholarship. She infuses motivational and perspicacious teachings with a sense of history and contributions of modern thinkers and teachers. She is a mother, setting the example and leading the path for her four amazing children; Tatiyanna, Shaleik, Naseyah, and Nacyiah. Her children have pushed her and encouraged her, as she completes her God-given assignments. Chemeka strives to building a foundation for her children to be trailblazers and powerful leaders, who will help to make a difference in the lives of others and impact their communities.

Chemeka is a minister, serving in the House of Mandate, located in Roanoke Rapids, North Carolina. She serves under the tutelage and leadership of her Pastor and Spiritual Father, Pastor Orin Perry. She is a CEO of I AM PURPOSED COACHING LLC, COO of Mandate Enterprise, nonprofit founder, author, *serial* entrepreneur, philanthropist and seasoned humanitarian. Chemeka is recognized as an African American woman, courageously pushing to help change situations for women and children who have faced domestic violence and/or abuse. She has a strong commitment to education, the empowerment of women economically and meaningful leadership. Chemeka has assisted more than 5000 women & children in crisis, by distributing free clothing, personal care items and food. She has single-handedly initiated and coordinated numerous corporate & community outreach programs and much more.

Chemeka received her B.A in Elementary Education from North Carolina Central University, Master of Arts in Counseling from Cambridge College, and in 2015 her Ed.S (Educational Specialist in School Administration) from Cambridge College. While serving for 13 years as an educator in public and private schools, Chemeka has also held numerous community roles. Chemeka served as Town Commissioner of Garysburg, NC and managed the Parks & Recreation Department for four years. Chemeka also served on several boards, including the Town of Garysburg Community Development Corporation, Board of Roanoke Valley Adult Day Center, and Department of Public Safety (DPS) of Women Correctional Institution for several years.

Chemeka also launched Pearls of Purpose, Inc, a world-wide feminist organization, for women of all ages. Pearls of Purpose, Inc focuses on women and children of domestic violence and abuse, families affected by incarceration, women and children facing homelessness and human trafficking. Chemeka's ambition is to empower families affected by abuse, incarceration and homelessness by providing information, programs and resources, to help them heal and live better lives. In 2018 Chemeka launched I AM PURPOSED COACHING, LLC- a global business and leadership Coaching Company. Chemeka also serves as the Chief Operations Officer of Mandate Enterprise.

Chemeka recently received the title of 2019 Ms. Black North Carolina, with a platform entitled, "DOMESTICALLY DIFFERENT!!!" This title grants her opportunities to become actively involved in the lives of battered and neglected women and children. As she interacts with the community, Chemeka stands boldly on the word of God, to relate to her listeners. Chemeka serves by advocating, educating and fighting to bring an awareness to end domestic violence and abuse. She fights to be a VOICE TO THE VOICELESS, STRENGTH FOR THE WEAK, AND COURAGE FOR THE SCARED!!!

Chemeka is a woman on the rise; impacting lives globally. As a result of her dedication and commitment to the up-building of people and communities, Chemeka was nominated by ACHI Magazine as the 2018 Community Leader of the Year. Chemeka has dedicated her life to bring awareness, educate and advocate for those affected by domestic violence and abuse because she endured abuse for many years and survived this silent killer. She desires to be the salt of the Earth and impacting lives wherever her feet may thread. She is LEADING ON PURPOSE!!!

In collaboration with her business partners, Chemeka facilitates entrepreneurship seminars throughout the nation. The seminars are provided to educate and inspire those who dream of owning their own business. Chemeka strives to provide alternatives for establishing and maintaining financial stability in uncertain economic environments. Chemeka's insights in leadership, facilitating your purpose and women's empowerment and advocacy have allowed her to help hundreds of women move from surviving to OVERCOMING life on PURPOSE!

Connect with Chemeka Turner Williams, B.A, M.Ed., Ed.S:

Certified Business and Leadership Coach
CEO-I AM PURPOSED COACHING, LLC
FOUNDER- PEARLS OF PURPOSE INC.
MS. BLACK NORTH CAROLINA 2019

chemekaturnerwilliams.com
chemekaturnerwilliams@gmail.com
919-348-9323

OVERCOMING THE SECRET PLACE

He loved me with his killer words, he loved me as his prisoner of war!! I was walking around hiding secrets of what was my reality. Trying to mask the pain of the scars and bruises. Trying to camouflage the black eyes and bruise marks around my neck. Tattered from head to toe in black and blue, like a gaudy outfit. Feeling ashamed; hoping no one would find out what was going on in my secret place. I endured and suffered because I was too fearful and ashamed of what my life had become. Embarrassed and self-conscious in my own skin; I tried to understand how did I ended up like this. How did it begin? How did it get this far? I was in too deep, to find a way out. Broken and abused, by the man I gave my heart to; broken and abused by someone I loved and shared my life with. What started as a love story, had quickly turned into a nightmare! The person that I thought was my knight-and-shining-armor ended up being my Dr. Jekyll and Mr. Hyde.

We met at the young age of seventeen. He was my high school sweetheart; my first love. This young man was so charming and charismatic! You remember your first love, at that age. He was just what I thought I needed and wanted. For a young girl, like myself, needing to escape the heavy weight I bore from pressures and responsibilities of premature adulthood, combined with abandonment issues, daddy issues, and having been molested, he seemed like a hero. He appeared to be my safe place, my way out of all the craziness that had occurred in my life at an early age. I thought I had met the "someone" who would love me to life. Little did I know, I was looking for love in all the wrong places. I was a young girl embarking upon a new journey of love and excitement, ready to conquer this path called life. Being full of love, I was ready to give love in the same manner, fully & completely. I did not understand this relationship would leave an everlasting impact on my life.

I jumped into a relationship quickly, eager to experience security and the desire of being a normal teenager. I was trying to escape the adult roles and responsibilities that had been placed on me. The fantasy was short-lived. I found myself living in a secret place. Silently screaming for help!! Each day, I became more bitter and angry. When I combined my anger with the garment of shame that I was now used to wearing; shame of being misused and mishandled physically, emotionally and sexually, the weight was heavy. I wore the label! You know the label we wear - not MK or Gucci, but "Damaged Goods". As a young woman, wearing this label, I was living in a confusing maze. I struggled to make sense of my feelings, frustrations, sadness and betrayal. Instead of having real "fun", I was "tossing and flossing," trying to fill the void heartbreak brings. To quote Aretha Franklin, *We search in desperation in all the wrong places for an escape that cannot be found.* This desperate search takes us down a dangerous road with no good end.

This is where my painful walk through abuse and domestic violence started. This began, what would be the worst years of my life! Him. My "escape." My "dream man." The young boy I met, would become the man who would terrorize me for almost 20 years. He had everything going for him. He was eloquent, dashing, and charismatic. People flocked to him with magnetic urgency. But this man died. The man I first fell in love with no longer existed. The Dream Man turned into a monster!

It didn't happen all at once, but slowly, day by day he'd take control of the little things in my life. Eventually, the abuse would occur more frequently and more severely. Once I fell under his spell, I endured much hardship and pain, before the spell was broken. My youth was "wasted" on someone who put up a facade and operated behind a mask.

It started out as jealousy and control. He would dictate where I could go, who I could talk to, how I would dress. Honestly, I thought it was cute at first. I would say things like, "he doesn't want anyone to have me", "he loves me that much" or "he just wants all my time and attention." I quickly learned this was not healthy. I felt suffocated by the grip he had on me and my every move. I began to feel isolated from my friends and family. Because I desired to be loved so badly, I overlooked his controlling behaviors. I started searching myself for ways to change my behavior and actions to make better please him.

Being young made me be more vulnerable to abuse. I was still trying to figure out what a healthy relationship was. I remember when I would make him upset or wore any outfit that caused me to get more attention, he would slap me, punch me, or call me all types of names. Many times, he would try to rip my clothes off to make sure I wasn't seen in them. My confidence and self-esteem began to decline. Insecurity started creeping in and I began to devalue myself. My self-love suffered.

Before this relationship, I had so much going for myself, academically and socially. I never imagined that I would subject myself to this toxic lifestyle. When he would drink, he would become even more abusive. I would always walk on eggshells; not knowing what to expect or what would set him off. I was always tensed-up, full of anxiety and fear!! I was mentally drained. There's no tiredness like the one you feel trying to masquerade. I would smile while hurting inside and out, and trying to hide everything from everyone! It was simply impossible to keep up the pretense!

I became pregnant in high school at the age of 18 with my first son, Jacquez. He was born prematurely and died. This sent me into a deeper depression. Part of me died with him. I had many people celebrate and rejoice in the death of my son. I was told by adults that I should be glad he died because having a baby would have messed up my life. During this time of mourning, my boyfriend and I became so close. He was there for me throughout all of my emotional breakdowns. I felt he was the only one I had who understood my pain. For months I saw a tender side of him. The side I longed to see was finally here. I forgot all about his previous aggressions towards me. Unfortunately, they resurfaced.

Yet, needless to say, I wanted another child. The loss that I suffered left a void in my life and I thought having another child would fix it. Months later, I became pregnant again, with my oldest daughter. As before, the fighting stopped. I knew that this was the change in him I was waiting for. I was deceived by my own desires. I can recall a particular day when my daughter was just a few months old and she was in my arms sleeping. We began to argue over what I thought was a minor issue. However, what I said made him upset and he began physically assaulting me, with my infant daughter in my arms! Instinctively, I covered her, to make sure she didn't receive any of the blows. I was screaming to the top of my lungs; enraged that he had no regards for our baby. A member of his family ran in the room yelling at him to stop. This did not make him cease. He continued to rage. The family member grabbed my daughter from me, to get her out of harm's way. I was so furious that I fought back with everything within me. With tears streaming and fists contracting, he eventually got off of me. I ran out of the room, got my baby and left the house. It was as if I was in a nightmare. He would call me, apologize repeatedly. He always said he didn't mean to do it and it was "the alcohol." I would distance myself from him for a few days and he would pursue me until he had my attention again. He would promise not to ever do it again and he insisted that he didn't remember the things he had done. I wanted to believe him, so I would blame the alcohol instead of him.

This cycle continued for years. One would think that I would finally leave, but I continued the relationship. Eventually I ended up *marrying* him, because I loved him and he promised that marriage would be different. Time proved differently. The sanctity of marriage caused no change in the evil he put down and offered no protection from his punishments. He would still knock me down, shake me, and push me into walls. The fights became more violent. The extremes of abuse I experienced were mind-blowing! From being the object of his adoration to being the object of his rage - he left no stone unturned. His behaviors revealed him to be the cold, heartless, merciless monster that he truly was.

Things elevated to such a severe level that it began to affect my livelihood. My employer was getting fed up with me missing numerous days of work. This was putting me in jeopardy of losing my job. Many times my "man" would show up at my job and try to make a scene. Desperately, I tried everything to keep him from exposing our secret to the public. I was holding this secret shame at a young age. Carrying it around like the grenade that it was. I was a ticking time bomb - hiding in plain sight. I was weighed down with depression, a broken spirit, hurt, angst, and at a loss for a will to live. I was God's piece of fine crystal, but at this point, you couldn't convince me of this. Instead, I carried myself as a broken and battered, discarded piece of glass, nearly destroyed by his constant abuse.

I now realize that as an abuse victim, I was at the whim and mercy of my abuser. I tiptoed on eggshells around his ever-changing moods and fickle feelings. I lived by constantly second-guessing myself instead of questioning the intentions of my dictator. As the victim, my "normal" consisted of living with the agony of not knowing what was coming next. Wondering whether I would be hugged, hurt, kissed, kicked, caressed or cursed? As the victim, I was like the proverbial frog in boiling water - I became so used to a hostile environment that I almost waited too late to make an escape; that was my life. My first questions of each day became- "Will I have to fight for my life today?".

Even pregnancy brought no empathy from him. During subsequent pregnancies, he put my head through a wall, stomped and kicked me with babies on the inside, covered me in bruises and drew blood. Jealous rages with guns drawn and pointed to my head became part of my "normal". The first time he beat me while pregnant, he choked me and pushed my head through a wall. I remember he aimed specifically for the stomach. I fought, trying to protect my babies. He kicked me over and over in the abdomen. I remember balling up in a fetal position just to protect my unborn babies.

I went to the doctor the next day, made up a story about how I'd fallen in the shower and I was worried about the babies. I had black eyes and swollen lips. They checked me with a sonogram and assured me everything looked fine, but even then I couldn't believe them. For months, I thought that since the beating had been so severe, surely something had to be wrong with the baby. And that fear became my reality. I was leaking amniotic fluid and was placed on bed rest. Fear of miscarriage or future complications added to my already stressed life. I felt guilty for not protecting my unborn children. Again, I had to lie to cover the violence of what really occurred. Lies became my normal!! Covering up the secret place that no one knew existed.

The attack on my unborn baby was my turning point. I had suffered from trauma and depression for years; I had planned my suicide to escape the pain. Fortunately, I switched to survival mode. I was convinced that by staying and surviving, I was at least able to protect my children from him. That night, I came to the realization that none of us were safe. I was left broken, defeated, and humiliated; standing to face a very difficult road alone. I should have died. Mentally and emotionally I did die. For a while, I held on by a spiritual thread. Yet through all this, I stayed.

The vicious cycle of abuse repeated and became a violent tornado. I was beaten within an inch of my life and finally called my brother for help. I knew that a brother finding his sister bloody and in such a shocking condition would undoubtedly unleash a rage, like no other! He called the ambulance. At the hospital, the police urged me to press charges. I was so reluctant to take that step, knowing that there would be hell to pay when he was released. Having my brother there to protect me gave me strength. It was NOW or NEVER! This time, it was LIFE or DEATH, my life and the lives of my children.

I knew that this thing would become public, and my facade of "peace" would be blown wide open! This was Chemeka - the beautiful one, the strong one, the smart one, college-bound young woman who had so much going for her. What would people think when they found this out? How would they respond? How would this affect my family and our reputation? What kind of life could we possibly have after this?

My abuser was a coward, preying on someone he felt bigger than. He threw the word "love" around like spare change. I felt trapped and paralyzed by his threats. What finally pushed me through to victory was his own indiscretion. He was arrested for another cause and had to serve a lengthy prison sentence long enough to provide my escape. I was still being subjected to abuse, even though he was not present physically. I was still being attacked mentally, emotionally and verbally. My life was ripped away from me and my children with had no warning. Now forced to become a single mother and a prison wife, I was at the lowest point I can ever remember. I had to endure even more fears, struggles, false judgements. A huge void was left in the hearts of my children. I fought daily to ensure that they didn't fall into depression, anxiety, and anger. It was time to let the healing begin. I now began the work to heal mentally, emotionally, and spiritually. Plagued by a world of hurt, suicide attempts, and options running out, I quickly saw that I could only run to God.

I am alive only by God's grace and mercy. God's hand allowed my survival. If I hadn't surrendered my life to God, if would of surely ended. Don't be deceived, it wasn't easy, and it is a process. It was a leap of faith, and faith without works is dead. I had to join my hand with God's hand to do this work and save my life and the life of my children! God has a mission for me and he also has one for each and every one of us in this life. He has equipped us with His power, but we must walk in it together with Him! Pity and power cannot co-exist within the life of a *saved* person. I realized that either I would be God's and be whole, walking in LIFE, or I would continue my "life" as the "walking dead". Even the great Martin Luther King said, "there comes a time when silence is betrayal"! I could no longer betray myself and my children, and all those who were in similar situations. The Light of God flooded my life and pushed through the darkness. I could now see God's glory awaiting, and the choices ahead of me. Chemeka had to choose, and she chose LIFE!

Although none of us want brokenness to define and identify what we may have experienced in our lives, quite often that is the path our journey leads us to. When our hearts are broken, our vision distorted, our lives are devastated and uprooted, our dreams turned to grief and pain, we must give it over to God. God wants to mend us and make us whole. He desires to heal us totally from our past scars and the pain that each one of us have encountered. There is no pain too great that God cannot heal. He heals the broken hearted, and binds up their wounds.

I now know that my pain had purpose. I have a better understanding of God's Word for the pain and suffering that we experience. Kingdom principles operate in a different realm and God has a plan for our brokenness. We may think or view our scars as a sign of failure, defeat, and unworthiness but that's not the way God identifies it. It's all about the perception and whose perception it is. What we perceive as insignificant and minute, God considers more than enough. God sees us in a different manner.

God Sees Beyond what we can see. It is true that we all have been scarred, but God sees beyond our scars, beyond our flaws, beyond the cosmetics we hide behind. He sees beyond our inadequacies, our insecurities, our failures, our hurts and tears. He sees beauty in our brokenness. He sees beauty in our ashes He sees a masterpiece being created. The world despises broken people and things, but God takes pleasure in using broken things. God demands that we be broken before He can even begin to use us. YOU OVERCAME ON PURPOSE!!!

You have healed and overcome to birth your destiny. You have overcome on Purpose so that destiny can come forth. God calls forth your destiny in the middle of your brokenness, in the middle of your pain, in the middle of your persecution, and in the middle of your suffering.

When you're redeemed, when you are restored, when restitution comes, you have a story to tell. You have a story that will save someone's life, you have a story that will free others out of captivity, and being abused. you have a story that will deliver others out of the hands of the enemy. You did not suffer for nothing. God never wastes pain. I have learned through God's Word to rejoice in our sufferings, knowing that suffering produces endurance, and endurance produces character, and character produces hope, and hope does not put us to shame, because God's love has been poured into our hearts through the Holy Spirit who has been given to us. (Romans 5:3-5 ESV) God allows crushing and breaking experiences that will cause us to look to Him. Often, God will use the things we love and feel we need, such as relationships, and vulnerable areas, such as our finances, to get our attention. God uses these broken areas, in our lives, to speak truth, to build strength, to build character, to cause humility and to draw us closer to Him.

There is beauty is your SCARS. Others saw flaws and God saw a pearl wrapped in PURPOSE. As for me, He has taken a broken, abused, messed up woman with many issues, and he is healing me, remolding me, and restoring unto me all that was lost and stolen. He is making me WHOLE. The pressure and weight of my pain created my pearl. A pearl must go through darkness, isolation, pressure, cleansing, and refining. It's a necessary process; the process where God begins to work on you and in you. The breaking and the pain had to take place. My battle scars and my pain were designed to let others see my transformation from SURVIVING to OVERCOMING and walking in my PURPOSE. Today, I can say, there is LIFE after abuse.

REFLECTIONS FROM AN OVERCOMER:

1) Put God First- When we think about God's word, it helps us bear some of the things we have gone through and the trials we face now. "*Accordingly, as his divine power hath given unto us all things that pertain unto life and godliness, through the knowledge of him that hath called us to glory and virtue.*" (2 Peter1:3 KJV) I came to the understanding that everything I needed to move forward and to heal, gain strength, and be restored was found by abiding in His word and seeking His face. I have to trust Him enough to be vulnerable with my brokenness.

The broken pieces were a blueprint for your PURPOSE!! God never changes!!! He is the same yesterday, today, and forever. When we place our faith, in Jesus, He reaches way down, from on high, and takes hold of us. Pray for the abuser's repentance. Pray that God will change their hearts and bring them into knowledge of their errors. Pray that God would protect *your* heart from anger and bitterness. Trust God and know that even in the darkest of days, He is still the light. God knows the truth, He sees all, He's all knowing. He will never desert you or leave you alone. You can rest in His care and know that vengeance belongs to Him. Jesus has the power and authority to restore and heal us from our broken past. He has the power to make us whole in Him. Satan wants to deceive us into thinking that God is blind to our pains, sufferings, and abuse, or he doesn't care.

REMEMBER THIS, God is NEVER blind to things that hurt His children. He grieves all sins and he hates them. Jesus understands abuse first-hand, he bore shame up on the cross. Jesus suffered the greatest abuse unto death so that WE may have everlasting life!! Give God your pain and allow Him into those deep dark secret places. Allow Him to mend the brokenness. You can be made WHOLE again.

2.) **Forgive yourself-** Forgiveness sets you FREE!! You must acknowledge that you were in an abusive relationship and that it was NOT YOUR FAULT. Nothing that you did or said warranted abuse. Stop blaming yourself for what happened, it was nothing that you deserved. Stop beating yourself up for the choices and decisions you made. You are not responsible for your partner's behavior and you must hold him responsible. You must understand that there are people in this world who will use cruel tactics to manipulate someone who loves them to get desired results. FORGIVE YOURSELF, pick up the pieces and move on. You must forgive yourself and get out of any abusive situation!

3.) **Love Yourself-** People who love themselves set boundaries. Learn how to say NO and mean it. This will build your self-respect as well as build up your confidence and self-esteem. Know your worth and your self-value. You are beautifully and wonderfully made. Even with all our flaws you are still God's beautiful treasure that deserves nothing but the best, never settle for less than you deserve. Loving yourself also means you can be particular with who you allow in your life. If an individual is not encouraging you to become a better and more prosperous you, limit or cut off all access to you. When you truly begin to love yourself you will demand love and respect from everyone around you. Also write down positive affirmations and say them out loud to yourself daily. Remind yourself of your value. Get involved in things that you love to do: Exercise regularly, eat properly, get adequate rest, journaling, all of these are just a few examples to help take back your life. Surround yourself with a good support system. Talking to others who have experienced abuse, can help you in your recovery process. You may also write down a list of people, in your life, who you are willing to talk with about what you are going through and what you are struggling with. Anytime you feel like you want to go back to your abuser, or experience feelings of guilt, call that trusted friend to help you get back on track. Take time to REMEMBER- you are not what happened to you, you are not your past.

4.) **Educate Yourself-** Learn the various types of Domestic Violence as well as the warning signs. Become familiar with the red flags that suggest a person may be potentially abusive. Pay attention to your instincts. Never overlook or minimize anyone's negative behavior towards you. Abuse starts simple and may be overlooked. Pay attention to repetitive behaviors, and DO NOT MAKE EXCUSES FOR THEM. Educate yourself on the laws in your state You have the right to be protected.

5.) **Seek professional help and spiritual healing-** There is no one-size-fits-all prescription for healing. This process varies depending on each individual and the level of trauma experienced. You need to seek a trained professional to assess your situation and your safety. The professional is trained to help you deal with emotional baggage from the past, mental and emotional state of mind, and to help you develop a strategy for change. Healing is not a quick process. It takes time. Healing is a lengthy, painful and emotional journey. You'll need help and professional guidance to walk through potentially explosive and destructive situations. It's imperative to seek Godly counsel. Reach out to pastors and church leaders in your community. Talk to them and make them aware of what you are dealing with. They can strategically walk you through the healing process. God is a HEALER!!! God invites us into his presence and transforms us by renewing our mind (Romans 12:2). It's imperative to spend time in God's word, prayer, worship, and fellowship. With professional help, and by following these principles, you can break the cycle of abuse in your life and begin your healing journey. As you reach out to God and others, you can experience God's redemptive purposes in your life and become a channel of healing in the lives of others. Make Jeremiah 29:11 your mantra: "'I know the plans I have for you,' declares the Lord, 'plans to prosper you and not to harm you, plans to give you hope and a future'."

Your SCARS tell a story. After so many battles faced; some lost and others won, you are standing here and with great strength. You survived what killed so many. No longer are you living in that secret place, NO MORE SILENCE, NO LONGER ASHAMED. You are SET FREE. Your PURPOSE was greater than your pain. Walk in your healing, walk in your newness, walk in your victory!! YOU ARE AN OVERCOMER!!

"He will rescue the poor when they cry to him; he will help the oppressed, who have no one to defend them. He feels pity for the weak and the needy, and he will rescue them. He will redeem them from oppression and violence, for their lives are precious to him."
–Psalm 72:12-14

Author

Valerie Staton Grant

Valerie Staton Grant

Valerie Staton Grant is a true Overcomer and a Survivor of Domestic Violence! Born October 8, 1969, Edgecombe County. She currently resides in Raleigh, NC, after living in Rocky Mount the majority of her life. Valerie is blessed to be the mother of two adult children, and grandmother of two grandsons.

Valerie currently works in the Program/Project Management field. She has been in this field for over 15 years. Valerie loves to travel and have fun with her family and friends. Valerie always has a positive attitude and doesn't mind going above and beyond to help anyone who is in need. Since 2015, Valerie has been a member of Raleigh North Christian Center (RNCC) and serves on the Greeter's Ministry.

By writing her story and sharing it with the public, her kids, family, and friends, Valerie feels totally free from everything. Valerie no longer has to carry the weight of abuse all by herself. She's totally free from all of the hurt, grieving, and pain of being unhappy. Life is so beautiful and this is the happiest she has been in a long time! Valerie prays that her story reaches someone's heart and convinces them that they too, can OVERCOME DOMESTIC VIOLENCE!

OVERCOMING THE DEMON OF A MONSTER

For over 15 years, I endured beating after beating from my ex-husband. It all started when my daughter was two years old; I was 20. My ex-husband was the type of man who would get mad about anything and want to start an argument. The first time he hit me, it left me broken and afraid. He blackened my eye that night and choked me. I was gasping for breath as he just stood back and watched. I called my aunt to come and get me. I packed up all of my and my daughter's clothes and left. My ex-husband begged me to come back so he could help take care of his daughter. I thought I was in love and ended up going back. Big mistake, as the beatings only got worse. He hit me one day and, in fear, I left and ran over to his aunt's house. He ran behind me and tried to beat me at her house. His aunt's husband stopped him. Things would be good for a while, then the arguments would start again; followed by the beatings.

In the midst of the good and the bad times, I got pregnant with my son. While pregnant with my son, my ex-husband beat me because he couldn't find an insurance check that I had put away for safe keeping. Instead of calling me and asking, where I had put the check, he tore up the bedroom looking for the check. When I got home, he was in a fit of rage and despite the fact that I was pregnant, he beat me. Fortunately, his dad intervened and stopped him and told him, "She is pregnant; don't hit her!" I never understood why someone would get so upset with you that they could resort to hitting you. I guess that's the demon side coming out.

I remember one time my ex-husband and I were riding down the highway in Rocky Mount, North Carolina, near Gardner's Barbecue; and it was very dark, cold and the rain was pouring down. We got into a bad argument. He stopped the car and dragged me out and left me walking down the street in the pouring rain.! I was so cold and afraid. He came back to get me a few minutes later and apologized. I still stayed because I was afraid of him; too afraid to leave. I never thought that in my life, I would be in an abusive relationship with anyone. Don't get me wrong, I did have a mouth on me. but only to defend myself. At the time, I loved my ex-husband, I would do anything for him.

A few years later, we moved, from Rocky Mount to my hometown of Dunbar, North Carolina; where we located near his mom and my grandmother. I never knew what mood he would be in when he came home. One day I was sitting at the computer doing my schoolwork; I was enrolled in online classes at Strayer University, working on my bachelor's degree. My work at the computer stopped when we began arguing. The argument became heated and he began hitting me; over and over again. The Sheriff was called to our home, but he only made my ex-husband leave to calm down. My mother had a scanner at her house and heard my address and cause of complaint over the scanner. It is so heartbreaking for your mom to hear something like that about her child. She came to my house to see what was happening and my ex-husband acted as if it didn't bother him at all, that she was there. His mom was there too and was talking to him about "putting his hands on me". The more his mother talked, the madder he got. No amount of talking could help him. I suggested going to counseling, and of course he was against it. It is so sad when your children have to grow up witnessing their parents fighting. My ex-husband never abused them, but they had seen too much of him abusing me. I had tried to leave several times, but I was never successful. I was afraid of him. It's so sad to live in a house that you are not comfortable in because you are always wondering if something bad is going to happen.

Another time that stands out in my memory, was when my ex-husband and I had a fight and my son and I had to walk down the street to his mother's house. My ex-husband had locked us out of our house. We stayed at his mother's house for a while, hoping that things would calm down. However, when we walked back home, we still couldn't get into the house and I needed to get clothes so my son could go to school the next day. I had my pocketbook and car keys, so I got in my car and my son and I stayed in a hotel for the night. My ex-husband knew where we stayed that night because he later told me that he rode around to see where we were. I didn't tell my mom because I had grown tired of telling her every time something happened.

I woke up one morning, having no idea that that day would be one of the worst days of my life. I remember being outside with my ex-husband and we were just sitting around talking. A woman called his phone and I could hear him making small talk with her. When he hung up the phone, I asked him who was that. He got mad and told me to not worry about it. No respect at all from him. So, I got quiet because I could see how mad he had gotten. That was when I, once again, realized that the Demon-of-A-Monster had come out! He started to curse me; calling me foul names. Then, all of a sudden, I was hit so hard! It took my breath away! I hit back because I didn't want to stand there and keep taking punch after punch from him. It was then that he dragged me into the nearby woods and started beating me, as if I was a man. I was screaming and hollering, but no one could hear me. The more I screamed, the further he dragged me into the woods. He kept beating me and dragging me until I went silent and passed out. No movement or anything, just still.

The next thing I remember was waking up on the couch with my children hollering and screaming over me- "What did you do to my mother?" What is wrong with her?" My ex-husband kept calling my name and crying because he didn't know if I was dead or alive. I knew that my kids didn't like the man their father had turned out to be. I couldn't blame them, as I didn't like the man he was either. I was at a point in my life that I really hated him. I couldn't stand being around him at all. Sometimes, I wished that he would just go away and never return. My children and I would have been fine with that; at least we would not have to worry or wonder if he was going to come home in a bad mood and fight me. He was always nice to others but treated us as if we didn't matter to him.

I was always running away from my home in fear; only to return again. But through it all, I knew that God had kept me. God was always protecting me. We stayed in that house for seven years. We lost that home and moved back to Rocky Mount. My ex-husband promised that he would never hit me again. That promise didn't last for long. There was a night when he wanted to have sex with me and I refused, so he raped me, and I pleaded and cried through it all. I couldn't bring myself to have sex with someone who treated me like I was nothing to him. I know that people may think it is crazy that I am saying that he "raped" me, but I did not consent and, - "no means no". It doesn't matter that it is your husband, boyfriend, or lover. He beat me so bad, put a gun to my head and told me that if I left him, he would kill me. I saw nothing but rage in his eyes. I was never happy. He never wanted me to go anywhere and didn't like me to speak to men who worked with me. If I spoke to them, when we got home, he would always start an argument and beat me. I was terrified. He could come and go and do anything he wanted to, and I was just supposed to deal with it. I never knew why I wanted to save my marriage after all he had taken me through. I was always trying to make it work for us; for our children as I never grew up with my father.

The year 2006 was the last year he abused me. My daughter was in high school and my son was in middle school. My ex-husband and I had gotten into a big argument about my going to Raleigh to a birthday party. He had a truck, a car, and a motorcycle. I had a SUV and was cleaning my vehicle. He called me and told me that he needed to use my vehicle and whatever it took to get the vehicle, he would do. I already knew what was going to happen, so I just kept on cleaning the SUV. He came in the yard, jumped out of his truck started an argument and started pushing me around while I was cleaning the SUV. I pushed him back and told him to leave me alone. He then took his fist and punched me in my eye and busted my lip and just kept on hitting me. I ran in the house into the bathroom as I could feel the swelling of my eye and lip. He came behind me and that's when my kids started screaming and yelling for him to leave me alone. He tried to choke me while I was in the bathroom. His eyes were blood shot red. You could see nothing but rage in his eyes. My kids and I ended up beating *him* that day! My son called the police to come to our home. Once my ex-husband realized that the police were on their way, he left in my vehicle. I had to call my mom to come and get us that night. My mom took me to the Magistrate office and I filed charges against him. They had a warrant out for his arrest because he fled. That Monday, his mother made him turn himself into the police so they wouldn't go to his job looking for him and causing him to lose his job. He stayed in jail for 72 hours. I had taken a restraining order out on him so he couldn't come back to the house. We were doing fine without him.

I don't know why I dropped the charges against him and let him come back and live with us. He begged and pleaded for me to drop them and he would never hit me again. I had heard that so many times. I was so numb to his lies. Yet, I let him return to our home. Our daughter graduated high school and moved to Greenville where she was going to school and working. She joined the Army in 2009. In 2010, my son graduated from high school and went to college. I never told my children, but I was never comfortable and couldn't be myself around my ex-husband He was never home as he was always running around with different women. I had gotten a really good paying job in Raleigh. I was working on getting our house refinanced. When I was in discussion with the mortgage company, the agent told me to only let my name stay on the deed and let my husband's name stay on the loan. I didn't understand why someone would tell me this. Later, it became the best advice that anyone had ever given me!

My son ended up joining the Navy in 2013. He graduated from basic training in January 2014. Little did I know that through my children's absence, God was preparing me to be alone. I ended up leaving my ex-husband and my house in May 2014. I walked away with almost nothing. Yet, peace of mind is a great substitute for being verbally and physically abused. I was able to get my divorce and since my name wasn't on the loan, I was able, for a small fee, to remove my name from the deed. God has always been with me even when I thought I had no one to turn to. I am so grateful for everything.

If you are ever in an abusive relationship; whether verbal, mental, or physical, please seek help and do not let the abuse keep going on. You are better than that and you deserve the best that life has to offer. I wish I had spoken up to my family sooner. I felt like I didn't protect my children and for that I apologize. My children and my grandchildren are my world. I love them to the moon and back. Don't deceive yourself. It's okay to let people know that you are not fine when you really think you are fine, over it, or just done. Take that time to heal and seek counsel and learn how to accept yourself and the truth as it is. You have to learn how to face your true identity and weaknesses as well as your strengths.

REFLECTIONS OF AN OVERCOMER:

As I close this chapter, I have five summary statements that I have taken with me-

1.) **Letting go to surrender**. Letting go is all about having *faith*. When I took the step to leave my husband, I finally stepped out on *faith*. I let God order my steps and lead me to become a happier person. I learned how to love myself and give love.

2.) **Freeing yourself from unhealthy emotions**. We've all felt pain before. It's like having a sharp knife piercing the core of your heart. Free yourself from unhealthy emotions by thinking positive thoughts. Surround yourself with positive people who will uplift you.

3.) **Learning how to be alone**. I knew that God was preparing me to be alone. I remember always being left at home by myself from 2010 – 2014. When I moved out by myself, I was prepared to live alone. It wasn't a good feeling in the beginning but as time passed, it was easier and easier. You learn so much about yourself. You learn that you can make it by yourself. Now don't get it confused, there's a difference between being lonely and being alone. When you're lonely, you have this emptiness inside that make you think about all sort of crazy things that are very painful. On the other hand, it is very good to spend time alone without interruptions; just your "me time" to relax, meditate and just enjoy being with only you.

4.) **Loving yourself enough to get through the recovery process**. You will have to humble yourself and give your entire life over to God. Pray about everything and stay encouraged so you can be a blessing to others

5.) **Paying Close Attention to your life.** You only have one life; and this life was given to you. It's a gift! You need to learn how to receive it each and every day. Embrace your family and true friends and remove all the haters from your life. Some people will just never like you regardless of what you do.

Author

Dana Underdue

Dana Underdue

Dana Underdue is a young lady with dreams way bigger than her eyes could ever see. Born in the small town of Gaston, North Carolina, Dana is a graduate of North Carolina A&T State University, with a B.S in business management. Dana truly believes in the Aggie Nation mantra that "Aggies Do." Dana is currently pursuing a B.S. in Organizational leadership and A.S. for Funeral Director. Dana is currently growing Due Insurance Agency, where she specializes in life, health, Medicare insurance and soon to add auto and home/renters' insurance. Dana also serves as an Executive Assistant to G2G Mentoring Services. One for true diversification, up and coming projects include her very own tow trucking company, D & D Towing, which will be based in the Virginia Beach and North Carolina areas. Dana loves sharing her multiple talents with the world, so this project is only the tip of the iceberg; be sure to keep your eye out for the uniqueness of Dana coming to serve a community near you! Dana is excited about life; recognizing for where God has brought her and where he is currently directing her path. Dana truly knows that with God, there are no limits!

OVERCOMING THE KNOWING

From an early age, we develop a mindset that distinguishes between things we like and don't like. Somewhere along the lines of maturity, we began to add into the mix of our personal "non-negotiables"- things we are willing to put up with and those things that we unequivocally will avoid or remove from our lives without a second thought. It is interesting... the evolution of our minds and thought process as we grow in life. Sometimes the things that we will not put up with become things that we use to judge others. This is where I found myself many times in this life of mine.

Growing up, I started out as a very enjoyable and outspoken person. However, as I got older, I steadily evolved into a very reserved child. The dynamics of my house consisted of my mother who is an alpha female and my father who is more relaxed and passive in nature. Early on, I took on more of my father's traits, as I began to mimic his calm, non-confrontational spirit. But like the two sides of a coin, the aggressiveness from my mother lay dormant beneath my surface- ready to be released if I was ever challenged.

My upbringing was what some may call "strict," some may call "sheltered," but what I now know to call "safe." If my mom let me stay overnight with anyone, she'd usually come and get me EARLY the next morning. I didn't get to go many places unless I was surrounded with family. There were sometimes that I was allowed to go out with friends; but it was limited to acquaintances that were the seeds of my mother's own friends. As an alpha female, my mother could be vicious with her words, but simultaneously had a heart of gold. Growing up in that environment played a major part in me becoming reserved. It also caused me to evolve into a rather spoiled child. You see, when my mom's aggression had been directed towards me, or when she knew she'd hurt my feelings, she would always buy me a gift. The gifts supplanted the apologies that never accompanied them. It became common for me to come home and find a gift on my bed; or she would just present the gift to me or simply give me money- all to mask what was had done. Sans the true apologies that I desperately craved, the outgoing me steadily slipped away and was replaced by a more reserved version of me I didn't really feel open to express myself because it was a challenge for my mother to accept my comments. So, a void was created in my life, as the person I loved dearly became someone with whom I couldn't share my true feelings, hurts, or pains. I soon learned to suffer silently.

Coming up in a well-known family presented a challenge for me. I grew up being told to "watch what you do," to "not shame the family name." I was hardly able to go out without someone asking me if I was an Underdue and being reminded of how great my aunts and grandmother were when they were growing up. The history that was established behind my family name made it hard to live in my area because I felt my life was always being watched and judged and compared to others. In my desire to not bring shame to the family name, I stayed clear of trouble and earned an image of being a "good girl." Unfortunately, this image also made me a target for secret hate. Friends and even family members had love-hate relationships with me. However, this wouldn't be exposed to me until later in life. One of my friends later told me that when I first tried to befriend her, she had avoided me. She explained that because I kept my hair done all the time and dressed well, she thought that I was "all that.". Being authentically me caused this friend to initially dislike and dismiss me. This taught me early on, that even the innocent can be found guilt; just being yourself can bring about an undeserved hate.

In college and during my early adult life, it appeared to me that the people who led wild, nonchalant lives all seemed to be the ones being blessed. Good things were always coming their way. I did not realize the difference between perception and reality; it could have been a mask that they were wearing. I was dazzled by the glitz and glam. My thoughts- "Here I am sitting here trying to be a 'good girl' and goodness is still avoiding me! I got to turn some things up!" Thankfully, it was just a thought because by this time, I'd gained too much wisdom from both watching and vicariously experiencing life through the suffering of my friends. Their experiences not only gave me wisdom, but they also helped shape the judgement that I'd need for my future chapters of my life. I watched my friends go through situations of serial cheating; situations that caused me to think how absolutely crazy they were! At times, I wished I could just say it to them. I watched them go through abuse... I would give advice to them to leave or run, but they'd always give the rebuttal of how much they "love him" and what they did to cause the cheating. I was always there for them... but eventually from a distance. I thought - "if that's what you want to put up with, you go right ahead!" In my mind, I'm like- "ain't no love going to make me do that; hit me once and I'm sending the squad to handle you!" Don't get me wrong, if you are a friend of mind, I hold you close, and I will have your back no matter what you decide. I just know after a while if we're talking about the same situation for the 50th time, my advice gets short and relegated to a mere listening-venting ear. I realized that real change only comes when people genuinely want it for themselves. I took so many mental notes of all the things I would never go through or allow to happen to me by watching some of my friends' lives. Funny how that still didn't keep me from the same traps.

As I got older, I looked and yearned for certain voids to be filled. At the end of my junior year in college, the bottom fell out of my comfortable life. I was shocked with a cancer scare; my mother was ill, and I was at risk of not being able to return to school due to lack of funds. These compounded issues filled me with fear, hurt and pain. It was during this valley moment that addiction was able to enter my life. Someone zeroed in on me and saw that I had a lot doing on; that my life was conflicted. They saw the pain behind my stone-cold face. That person offered to ease my pain and I was down with it. Smoking marijuana became life to me. I mastered sharing only what I wanted to and hiding the important things behind my new addiction. I began suffering in silence. I would over-indulge myself in my new coping mechanism. When high, I was able to escape the pain. However, this was only temporary; once the high was gone, the pain was still present.

I got to a frustrated space where I no longer cared. I was tired of not having the career, success and the love I wanted. I despised the fact that people who had no concern about upholding a decent image were achieving while I wasn't. In my desperation, I began listening to people talk about ways for me to make a lot of quick money. Suddenly, I was hooked on becoming a drug dealer, and my associates were more than willing to assist me in putting the puzzle pieces together towards my newly desired "career." I went from thinking of becoming a drug dealer, to thinking about becoming a madam! Like one needs a blueprint to build a successful building, I had acquaintances schooling me on the best locations to attract high-end clientele. While in the presence of my friends, I was hooked… but when I left the crowd and was by myself, I knew deep down that this lifestyle wasn't for me.

I was in a broken and lost place. The "light" in me was not the same. A friend saw my fragile state and invited me to church. As I started going to church, I started to regain some of what I had left behind a long time ago. As time went on, I still had voids in me that I wanted to be filled. I desperately craved love. It was not long before I found myself in a situation that I had no business being in. Despite all the mental notes and cautionary tales burning inside me, I found myself in the exact same place where I had once judged others. I had fallen into the same trap! I began dating a man who I had no business connecting with because of who he was and the obligations he had. This man was living a double life. Already in the relationship, I found out that he was a married man. This is where my family love-hate dynamics came into play. When one of my relatives heard of the affair, she took no time exposing it to my family. The exposure caused me to shy away from my family to avoid the looks and whispers.

From the beginning of the affair, "my new man" showed signs of being a classic abuser. However, I ignored the signs and laughed off certain things that he would do. It started with him taking his finger and pushing it in my forehead; telling me that I was his property or limiting where I could go. If I said something about other men or something he did not like, he would give soft slaps to my face. Again, abuses that I laughed off. Thankfully, God intervened in that situation by sending me a person who saw right through what I was going through and was able to make me put on my running shoes and get out of that relationship!

Still a broken woman, I was introduced to a very handsome man who wasn't physically abusive but who played mind games and lied. He was a true womanizer at its best. When I confronted him about suspected lovers, he chalked it up as "fake news" or simply things that had happened in his past. He told me everything I wanted to hear to keep me there; things like telling his family that I was his future wife. Even without a true commitment to marriage, I remained… confident that he'd soon get the epiphany that all he was looking for was right there in me. Of course, that day never came.

After that failed relationship, I found satisfaction in a form of self-abuse; I became an emotional eater. When I didn't get the love or attention that I longed for, I would find it in food. Food was absolutely satisfying! When everything else was failing me, food was there to pick me up. It was like eating good food became orgasmic to me! He didn't call, he didn't answer my texts, but when I got that cake or that candy and ate it, it gave me that warm feeling that I was looking for in that moment. As I continued my unhealthy relationship with food, trying to fill the void in my life, I reached a dangerous point. My weight had ballooned to almost 300 pounds!

Taking an overview of my life, I thought about the couple of times I could have been married. My immature thinking, my worrying about what others would say, and my worrying that I wasn't advanced in certain areas and wasn't good enough had sabotaged my opportunities. There had been good men who had the ability and wanted to love and help me through my past pains and hurt. However, I was use to hiding my truth and it left gaps in conversations. Conversations did not flow smoothly. As a result, several men received mixed messages. They thought I wasn't interested, when I really was! Missed opportunities. So, I decided that when the next opportunity came across my path, I would handle it differently.

Now, I was recovering and regaining a lot of my peace back. I was moving into what I thought was my complete healing, through the ministry and teachings of my new church. I met a guy, I thought he was cute, but once I realized his age, I thought, "Hmm, he is way too young, but we can be friends. I will make him my little brother." As we began to talk a little more, I realized that he was very mature. His age didn't even seem to match his intellectual level. The more we talked; the more feelings started to grow. He really had my attention, so much so that I found myself calling him whenever I had a chance. Even on my job, during my down time, I spent it talking to him. I mean he was so sweet. He would do things like ask a series of questions, then do something surprising with that information. Once he asked what my favorite cartoon character was and when we saw each other, he had a picture of bugs bunny drawn out! I thought it was so sweet how he paid attention to details and remembered things that were important to me. He wrote me poems all the time. When he expressed to me that he wanted us to be a couple, I thought- "No! He is just too young." Then a flashback played in my mind of the missed opportunities in my past when I had been judgmental and missed out on possible happiness. I did not give him an answer then. I waited a while. One day, I told him at the last minute that I was getting baptized. His car was broken down at the time, but to my surprise he found a way to be there! Right then I knew that I would make our relationship official and I did. When I came out after my baptism, he had a rose for me. It was so wonderful; this sweet, caring and loving young man. What I loved was when we were dating later in the relationship, he kept the fire and desire going at the exact same rate and passion level that he did when we first started dating. However, as time when on in this relationship, I started to see that he was a little controlling and had insecurities. Still, it didn't throw up a red flag.

My love for him just continued to grow. I thought that he was just being cautious and was afraid of getting hurt and so was I. Then he started giving me rules on different things that he did not want me to do. He wasn't a fan of conversations with your exs. I loved him and so I obeyed. However, he too had an ex; that he had a child with. So, his communications could not end with his ex. One day we were enjoying a movie together and he just blurted out in our conversation that he was a bad person and why did I want to be with him. I looked in his eyes and the glow that I normally saw wasn't there. He was serious, so we talked it out and then he said it, "I hit my child's mother." Astonished, I asked- "What do you mean?" He repeated it again- "I hit my child's mother." I rationalized with him- "Okay, well you are not that person now; that is not you. Just because you have done some bad things in the past, that doesn't make you a bad person." I was just thinking he thought that his sharing this would make me run. But I know anybody could change, so I took it as him sharing with me because he wanted me to know. I talked to him about God and the enemy and that what he did was wrong but not to let the enemy hold him there. So I felt good that he wanted to share this with me, So a month or so passed and he had this same look again, and again he talked about hitting his child's mother and I started my same talk but this time he said it happened a couple days ago. This startled me. He went on to tell me the things she did and said that made him angry enough to hit her. Still, no red flags went up. I just thought- he wouldn't do this to me cause that stuff she's doing I don't do. We talked it out and I told him to let it go and stop allowing her to take him to that place of anger. I encouraged him to continue to move forward. I never considered that there could be more to this; that the relationship must still have some strong feelings if he could still get that angry. Blinded by love, I ignored all the facts that were right in front of my face. Later, it became clear that he had hit the mother of his child multiple times and it had been going on for years; even during the first months of our official relationship. He thought I would leave but I wanted to feel love and give my love even more now that he was struggling with this problem that I thought I could fix. So, I stayed; I saw no reason to leave. Remember this is what *she* does, I don't do those things; I know how to act.

One night while I was sleeping, he woke me up out of my sleep and he was pointing to my phone and asking me about something he was reading. I rolled over and said- "It's nothing. Some things just transferred over from my old phone." He wasn't trying to hear that, so when I looked at what he was looking at, I woke up fast! It was texts from my last relationship; someone he most definitely didn't want me talking to! We texted months ago; around the time he told me not to talk to this past boyfriend again. Now, my new man wanted to see the *full* conversation. By this time, I was all the way up; heart racing, trying to remember exactly what was discussed in the text. Now, he is yelling, and I am panicking. He is yelling- "OPEN THE PHONE NOW!!!" I had never seen him this angry! It was at this point that I had a flashback to our conversations, and I remembered that he hit women! So, I was trying to open the text but afraid of what would be found that he might not like; innocent or not. It was the fact that no communication was the order; I was to obey. I was, shaking and trying to calm him down, as he was trying to snatch the phone. We struggled against each other as I tried desperately to hold on to the phone. As I got backed up to the door, I felt my breath leaving my body and my knees shaking. All the time he was in my face yelling for me to- "OPEN THE PHONE!!!" I saw his hands ball up and raise. I was scared; I closed my eyes and heard a LOUD BANG, when I opened my eyes and looked to the left, I saw his knuckle prints dented in the door. He didn't hit me; he hit the door. I was relieved and thought- "Wow, he loves me because he could have hit me, but he hit the door!" Crazy how in my mind, I found renewed confidence and believed that he loved me because he had hit the door and not me. He was pissed and threw all my clothes that I had packed to come over, out the house on the ground; all my stuff. He wanted me gone, but it was around 2 am and I lived in a different city, so I wasn't planning on leaving. We were able to get pass that part. Part of our getting on past that moment was for me to block this person from my phone and from my social media pages. It didn't stop there. Every man that I had talked to before was put on the block list, but not just blocked on my phone. I had to call the phone company and get them to block the number as well. Even though I didn't cheat he just did not allow the whole ex-boyfriend part. Now I knew it more than ever; that rule had to be obeyed.

In the course of our relationship we became engaged.; only for it to come to an end because of his conflicted situation with his ex, the mother of his child. He still loved her but now he had developed love for me. We had a time of separation. Months later we got back together. However, the things he said didn't match his actions. He told me he was not in a relationship with the mother of his child; she was just coming to drop off their child. Yet, he moved my car so she would not know that I was there at his house. When I questioned him, he just said- "I am single, but she don't need to know my business, okay". So, when she got there to drop of the child, she started to come up the stairs, saying it must be somebody here and once he realized she was coming up the stairs, he grabbed her. I couldn't see the full interaction, but I knew that something was happening. Yet, I didn't leave once she left; I stayed. Still in my mind, I am thinking- "Wow, she is still going through that abuse and still allowing him the time of day. Just leave him alone. She is crazy". I know… I had all the red flags in the world; yet, I still stayed.

The back and forth continued until finally I found myself once again in a situation that I said I would never be in. He and I were playing around one day and my phone became a topic and he asked to see my phone. When we had been separated, an ex-boyfriend that I had not seen in about six years sent me a message. When we got back together, I told him about the message from the ex-boyfriend and that I deleted it. Now, he was checking my phone. My nerves were becoming anxious because I didn't know if he would see something that would offend him. To my regret, I soon saw that the message I had deleted was sitting in my clipboard! I was made aware of how he felt about it when I received punches in my side and thigh! I thought what is going on. He is yelling about the conversation I had with my ex-boyfriend. Then punches to the other side of my body. In shock, I jumped up out of the chair, while he was yelling and getting angrier. Suddenly, I found myself in a chokehold and I was trying to pry his arms from around my neck. I was in a panic and I couldn't breathe! In my mind, I played back all the times I said that what was happening to other battered women would never happen to me. Then I thought of everyone that I had ever judged for dealing with this type of treatment. While in this chokehold, I asked to be forgiven for having been judgmental. I was still trying to fight free, when he suddenly let me go. He got his stuff and left. I know you may be thinking, - "Okay, so she calls the police to handle that." No, once he left, I could feel my sore spots that would turn into bruises. I'm yelling; talking to myself- "I can't believe he just did that; I love him, I don't want him to leave because of this." I hopped right in my car and went after him. I know that sounds insane, but I searched until I found him at the gas station. At the gas station I was telling him to come back and I was apologizing for everything. Finally, he came back to the house. The relationship was still rocky after this incident, but he had a talk with someone who made him realize how much he had put me through. He came to my house and apologized and explained that he wanted to make our relationship work. H said he wanted to be the man I always wanted; I was so happy. That was all I wanted, and it was such a romantic scene. It began to rain as we kissed, as if to symbolize a fresh, new start. That new start was short lived. A week or so after the *new beginning*, I saw that he was texting his ex and so I tried to see what type of business he was handling with her. He got upset. I was trying to talk with him to let know I wasn't mad; I just wanted to know what was going on. By this time, he was playing a game on his phone. I was playfully grabbing the phone so he would listen to me; not mad, had a smile on my face. He saw my actions as a show of anger and swung at me and hit my eye. Then he was punching me and somehow, I fell on the floor. I got up off the floor and I found myself swinging back and it came to my mind that this is not me and somehow, I slipped and fell down to one knee and I cried out- "Lord, I repent for everything I've done. My abuser heard me and stopped and told me to get out. I was still trying to explain that it was all a misunderstanding. Again, all my clothes were thrown out. All my possessions were cracked; as I was.

REFLECTIONS OF AN OVERCOMER:

1. **Seek GOD in all things!** I began to find myself when I found God and allowed him to repair the broken pieces in me. I tried allowing my voids to be filled by people, places and things, but I quickly learned that I must look to "the hill from which cometh my help." I truly needed God. I realized that no love is greater than the love of our Father. He is the healer of all things.
2. **You must take the time to heal.** Everything, you experience in your life, can become building blocks to something bigger if you don't take the time to heal from it if first. Once I was able to heal the front side of my heart, it allowed God to work on the back side of my heart as well. I began to love me again. It was hard to forgive, but I prayed and prayed and prayed to have a heart to forgive. I prayed to forgive all who hurt me, all who wronged me, and most importantly, to forgive myself. I found myself opening up to my mom and we are now able to work on our relationship, which is now growing in a new and beautiful way.
3. **You have the power to speak LIFE!**. Watch the things that you say because life and death are in the tongue. You decide if you are speaking life or death. Speak your future not your funeral.
4. **You can't change people!** As I healed, I learned to honor others as well. I learned the importance of not judging others, because you can easily be put in that same place within a matter of seconds. My healing also helped me to truly SEE others. In the words of Maya Angelou, *"If someone shows you who they are, believe them the first time."* Even if you can see the good in a person, don't ignore their faults. Remember that only God can cause a person to change and in order for that to manifest, he or she has to want it. Never pursue a relationship thinking you can change someone. It ends up leaving you depleted, confused and lost. Your peace is not worth that stress.

5. **Know your worth & don't be afraid to seek help.** One thing you must remember in healing yourself is that you must be opened to getting help, when needed. I thank God for having a spiritual leader that I can pray with. Don't be afraid to seek out leaders and experts to help you heal and move forward.

   Finally, always know your worth. Know who you are and never compromise your standards, if someone cannot rise to meet you; you rise up for yourself. Know it's okay if things are not moving as fast as you want them to. In the words of Priscilla Shirer, "*God has a place that is reserved for you and it's just waiting for you to get there, a place that has your name on it.*" No matter the mistakes you have made in life, you can and you shall overcome... Claim your victory and break the silence, be healed from the knowing.

Author Tasha Jones

Tasha Jones

Tasha Renee' Jones is an Overcomer in every sense of the word. However, the journey to get to victory has not at all been easy nor pretty. By the age of four, her parents had divorced, and she was left in the custody of her mother. Tasha's mother, having been rejected by her own father, abandoned, ridiculed, and abused as a child herself, became Tasha's first abuser. This was the beginning of a vicious cycle of *survival.* Tasha experienced child abuse very early in age; having suffered at the hands of a child molester from age five until age seven. This trauma led to a lifestyle that was dangerous and eventually spiraled out of control.

In search of validation, attention, acceptance, and worth, Tasha began "looking for love in *all* the *wrong* places." She was like forbidden fruit; the exotic dancer, the "mistress" to married men, and a "trophy girl" to men and women alike, who could afford to spoil her with expensive gifts and trips. The look of luxury and of glamour was very deceiving and came at a much higher cost than she could have ever imagined. Tasha lived a life that led to dark places and escalating desperation. Amid chaos, Tasha found herself in the arms of her "Prince Charming. Believing in the fairy tale, she fell completely in love with him. Seeking rescue; she hoped to finally be swept off her feet by this man that she could call her own. Unfortunately, what awaited for her was the paralyzing grip of a narcissist who ultimately attempted to destroy her.

For nearly 16 years, Tasha suffered mental, emotional, psychological, and physical abuse from this man who professed to be in love with her. Seeking to maintain her lifestyle and career in Corporate America, she learned to "save face", and became the "Master of the Mask". Depression, anxiety, Post-Traumatic Stress Disorder (PTSD) and even a failed suicide, were all cloaked in designer clothes, expensive shoes, a beautiful home, luxury cars and frequent vacations. It was in this, the darkest place and the deepest of hurts, that Tasha began to seek for "Help" ….

Then "HELP" showed up; His name is Jesus Christ. It was HIS Spirit that drew her out of the darkness and into HIS unconditional and unfailing LOVE. It was in HIS arms that she came to understand that she was Broken. Yet, she was Beautiful, and most importantly, she was HIS and nothing that had been done to her, nor by her, was greater than HIS Love for her.

Tasha Jones is now an Ordained Evangelist, servant and mother to her beautiful daughter, Jaidan. She is also the wife of Daryl Jones, a man who loves Jesus. She is the Founder and CEO of Broken Beautiful, LLC and Broken Beautiful Ministries, where she is an ICF Accredited Life Coach/Christian Mentor. She is the visionary of SHIFT ~ Sisters Healing in Christ Together Life Group where she teaches and demonstrates to women their value according to God's Holy Word.

In every facet of life and ministry, Tasha's divine purpose is to help those that were just like her, to know that they too, are Broken and Beautiful and there is an amazing "after this" waiting on the other side of their new life.

Connect with Evangelist Tasha Jones:
FB: Evangelist Tasha Jones
IG: IAmBrokenBeautiful
BrokenBeautifulllc@gmail.com

OVERCOMING PRINCE CHARMING

Then along came my "Prince Charming"; and charming he was. We met in a private party that I'd been hired to host. He had a friend approach me and say, "My man would like to talk to you," and pointed over in his direction. Me, with my smart and sassy self, replied, "Your Man wants to talk to me? Doesn't he have a mouth?" I was smart mouthed, especially to men in the strip clubs and the private parties, because I had no respect for them. I was there to get money and I knew how to get it. I was the Queen of running game. So, when the so-called friend approached me and not some "trick," I must admit, I was intrigued. So, I told the friend to have "his man" come over and talk to me. He did.

We talked for HOURS. There was never a dull moment in the conversation. I felt so comfortable talking with him; like I had known him all my life. He was well dressed, smelled good and was smooth. I was a sucker for dark chocolate skin, pretty teeth, exotic cars, nice attire and "good" shoes. And the fact that he had proper speech and could articulate a sentence with depth.... CHILE.... I was so messed up. He had a strong northern accent, which I loved. At the end of the night we exchanged numbers and a passionate kiss. We would stay in contact so we could see each other again. After speaking on the phone for a while, the conversations seemed to be getting sweeter and more captivating. I wanted to spend all my time waiting for his calls.

Maybe two months into our lengthy and "fairy-tale" like phone calls, he told me he was planning to visit. I was as giddy as one experiencing a school girl's crush. He would be my "Love" and the first *REAL* relationship that I had. Sure, I had companionship with other women's husbands, but I never had a man of my own. I was mesmerized. I was unguarded because he appeared different. We had amazing times. He made me feel like I'd never felt before. His language was beautiful towards me. He bought expensive gifts and took me shopping. I was falling for him. He would call me his "fantasy girl" and even though I had heard that before from other men, with him, it sounded genuine. I was everything that he'd dreamed of and I was "*all his*".

I was still dancing and doing private parties. The money, attention and power were addictive, and truth be told, I was still seeing the married man that I'd been having an affair with for over five years. The "Married Man" was funding my living and traveling; he was also my friend; the one I trusted. I was making enough money to pay my bills, but the condo and car were his. I had to keep him around and be his "Trophy" too. But I was falling for this new dude. I couldn't tell my new guy about "Married Man", because he would leave me, too. I'd miss out on everything that I wanted and desperately needed from him. I needed to be loved and I needed HIM. About a year into our courtship, he called to let me know that he was moving down south, and he wanted to be exclusive. We'd been having the most amazing times together. So, I cut everyone that I was dealing with; including my "Friend".

My New Dude was the "jealous" type, but in a "cute" way. I was still dancing after moving in with him. One day I was packing the car to leave. I walked to the door to kiss him bye, and he snatched me... That was the first time. The look in his eyes was evil. He had a smirk on his face as if to say, "I got you now". The fear that tormented me as a child was the SAME fear that gripped and paralyzed me right where I stood. Immediately tears streamed down my face. He loosened his grip, wiped my eyes and began to apologize for scaring me. He said he was falling in love and didn't want me to leave him. This was the beginning of the "I'm sorrys". He appeared remorseful for his actions. His apologies looked identical to my mother's... buying gifts. The red flags should have sent me packing. The familiar gut-wrenching emotions and fear should have been enough. But I stayed.

Things only got worse. I quit dancing and got a job in corporate sales. I would obviously meet new people daily because I worked in the public. Anytime that he and I were out together, and someone spoke, especially a man, I would get asked how I knew them. I was an account manager for the city and had many males' numbers. It got to the point that he would accuse me of "seeing" them. By this time, between the beatings, fights and pure hell, there would be those few weeks that would slip in to remind me of our beginning; when he was "in love".

I was stalked by the man that I married! We were three years in and married. I had a corporate job, wore business suits and our mutual friends could have never imagined the abuse. He let me know that if I told, he would kill me. I've had guns put to my head. Besides, how embarrassed and humiliated I'd be if people knew! If I didn't know anything else in life, I knew to keep secrets. The abuse was hidden with a new home, nice cars, beautiful jewelry and expensive attire. He was not at all, even remotely, close to the façade that he displayed. He was a narcissistic womanizer. He hated his own mother. I could tell by his language and the names he called her. He was a compulsive cheater. He was the type that even when things were going well for a while, he would cause a fight to have an excuse to leave to be with other women. I knew it from the very beginning. When his "girlfriend" called his house and I answered the phone he told her that I was his sister. I was so desperate to be loved. I accepted whatever was thrown at me with the "hope" that I could change him.

Four years into our marriage, a new home and a baby girl. The beatings and the fights are not what they used to be, however there are still arguments and manipulation. The physical abuse isn't like it was; but the verbal, emotional and mental abuse never ceased. Around others, we were the quintessential family living the American Dream. The beautiful portrait of a multi-racial family. The lies and deception. I had befriended a gentleman that worked in law enforcement. He knew the woman that my husband was sleeping with. She was my husband's girlfriend from years ago and they continued to see one another for many years. This person took an interest in me in the way of looking out for me. He never tried to come on to me.

One morning he sent a graduation photo of himself with the caption "Good morning Beautiful". I didn't even know that photo existed until I was awakened by my own screams. I was snatched by my hair out of bed and drug across the floor to my living room. I was hit across the head repeatedly with a wrought iron candlestick from my coffee table. I was punched in the face and stomped. My head lay cut open and my ear drum busted. I screamed for my life. I had no idea from where this rage was coming. It wasn't even 7 AM. I don't know how long the attack lasted. I must have blacked out a few times because I felt drunk and tremendously dizzy. I remember thinking, I cannot die and leave my baby. I was terrified to fight back. All I could think about was my baby. I didn't want someone to find me in my home badly beaten or dead. I had to save myself. He was standing over me, I'd slid from him to get from under him and found myself pressed against the front door with nowhere to go. He had full advantage to kill me from this point. I remember the look on his face. It wasn't even human. It was totally black, red eyes and foam coming from his mouth. His screams sounded like growling. All I could muster under my breath to say was, "GOD, please don't let me die."

It felt like an eternity laying there. I heard my baby cry. It was a cry that I'd never heard before. He stopped. He went to get her and when he did, I didn't know where the strength came from for me to get up, grab the phone from the kitchen, get to my bedroom, lock the door behind me, get to my bathroom to dial 911. I was scared to speak, but I whispered, "He is going to kill me". I heard him banging on the bedroom door; then I heard the back door close and I saw him leaving with my baby! I thought that he'd harm her. I begged the 911 operator to get someone there immediately.

I lived in a rural area and knew it may take some time to get to me. Now, I wasn't afraid for me, I was afraid for my baby girl. This was the worst I had ever experienced with him and we'd been together for 10 years at this time. This was 2006 and I was a Mommy, not just a mother, and I was going to fight with everything in me for my baby. I went before the judge this same day, in total humiliation, covered in blood, in a courtroom full of people for an emergency ex parte order. My life was in danger and so was my baby's. I was granted the order and removed from my home, even though the property was in my name. He was my husband and still had a legal right to the property and I would have to obtain an eviction notice to have him removed, even in this situation. So, I had to take a Sheriff with me to remove our personal items. I had to live away from him. He couldn't be found within 100 feet of me or our daughter. He couldn't contact me in any way. This did not stop him. He'd get his best friend to call, or use his phone to call me crying, begging and telling me how sorry he was. Again, the apologies, the false humility and the fake remorse.

For four months I lived elsewhere. He'd even convinced his best friend that he "can't live" without his family. He convinced his mother to reach me to apologize on his behalf and she made excuses for "why he is the way he is". He sent expensive bouquets to my job with handwritten cards, which he'd never done before. He was doing everything to prove that he had changed and wanted his family. So, I moved back in. But I was not the same. I was checked out. Emotionally disconnected. The gifts and the sweet gestures meant NOTHING TO ME ANYMORE. I was fearful, but in a different way. My fear had turned to anger mixed with anxiety and depression. My goal and reason to live was to protect my daughter. I lived with memories of being beaten severely in my own home; the evil one that stood over me saying, "I'll beat you to a pulp. Your own family won't recognize you. Bitch! I'll kill you". I lived with the terror of being stalked and threatened with guns.

I lived every day of my life remembering the rage he unleased on me. I remembered him chasing me down Interstate 95 with my baby in the back seat of his truck, trying to run me off the highway with speeds up to 80 miles per hour. I remember that day, a couple on 95 noticing the erratic driving and getting their little white Toyota Corolla between us and driving right up on my bumper after I motioned for help. They called Highway Patrol and I was able to safely take an exit. I felt better about being safe, but my daughter was still in his vehicle. Then I got the text, "Your Guardian Angels saved you TODAY". There were so many disgusting and evil thoughts that were attached to being in that house. I was always on edge and unfortunately, I expected something to happen. Even when things seemed okay.

There was no turning back for me. We slept in separate beds and lived as roommates. I wanted nothing to do with him. I wanted him dead. I had contemplated many days and nights of just "how" I would take his life. He'd stripped me of mine. I had no identity with him. Not one of his friends even called me by my name; I was known as "His Wife". I would sit on my sofa, gun in hand, and meditate on how I could blow his brains out when he entered the back door. In my mind, he would never know what hit him and I could plead insanity. There came a point, while I struggled with anxiety and depression, that I was clinically diagnosed with Post Traumatic Stress Disorder (PTSD). I know this may be graphic, but the hell that I lived for nearly 14 years was real. Everyone has a breaking point. And I had reached mine.

I began to pray and question GOD on my existence. I questioned HIM on my reason to live. I questioned my parents, the abuse, the abandonment, the rejection, the trauma, the torment. I was angry with my Creator and blamed HIM for everything that had been done to me. I blamed HIM for every hit, every word spoken over me. I blamed HIM for anxiety, depression, PTSD, miscarriages and all the hell... I blamed Almighty GOD Jehovah for everything. I even questioned that if HE was my Protector, why didn't HE protect me. Why did HE allow some nasty sick man to molest me? Why didn't He stop my Mother from abusing me? WHY DIDN'T HE LOVE ME ENOUGH TO STOP ALL THE PAIN?

I said to Abba Father, one day while driving, "Father, You said that If I should ask anything from You, In the Name of JESUS, You would do it. So, I'm asking You to save me. I don't know what it looks like and I truly don't even know what it means, but You say in YOUR

WORD that YOU are My Deliverer. Will you deliver me from this evil? In Jesus Name, I beg You, Jehovah. Please deliver me. If You don't, I will die." I began saying this prayer every day; on my 25-minute commute to and from work. I would pray and cry and I would not stop begging.

It was nearly 3 years later; the beatings had stopped, and we were cordial towards one another. There were still the sarcastic remarks and the nit-picking to cause an argument, however, not even close to the intensity of before. I started reading and "studying" GOD's WORD and seeking HIM more than ever before, during those 3 years. I was desperate to live and during this time I was having Encounters with The Holy Spirit. I didn't know it then. In 2010, the third year of my seeking GOD daily for myself and my daughter who was 5 at this time; my husband was arrested and sentenced, the following year, for a jail term of seven and a half years for conspiracy. Although, I had prayed for deliverance, and he reminded me of it once he went to prison, this was not at all what I expected. I lived imprisoned in my own home, so I was not thinking that this was deliverance. But it was. Not just for me and our daughter, it was for him also. I thought it would be a wake-up call for him and might even change him. I thought for sure, he will give his life to Christ now that he has nothing but time to focus on getting the Help that he needs. That hasn't happened for him; however, it is my prayer for him, still to this day.

Being married to a narcissistic personality is debilitating. It will drain the life out of you and will attempt to kill you mentally, physically, emotionally and spiritually. I was always at fault for his behavior. The same things that he "lusted" about me, it was never love, were the exact things that he hated about me and used to tear me apart.

REFLECTIONS OF AN OVERCOMER:

1.) Love yourself first- Learn to love you first, by learning GOD's love for you. I am not what happened to me, what others have done to me, nor what I have done to myself. I AM a child of GOD and I AM a Daughter of The King. I AM Royalty. My identity is found in HIM. I AM no longer Surviving in Silence. I AM AN OVERCOMER. I am no longer angry with GOD and I blame HIM for nothing. I endured this so that my daughter, you and your daughters won't have to. I broke the generational curse over my family forever and you can too.

2.) **Trust your intuition**- If you have an uneasy feeling about someone, don't discount it.

3.) **Heed the red flags**- If the "red flags" are waving, please heed the warning that danger is present.

4). **It is not okay-** If anyone ever puts their hands on you in any unwelcomed way, do NOT pretend that it's okay and do not accept, "I'm sorry." They will watch your reaction and if unchecked, will do it again; worse.

5.) **Recognize the abuser-** And lastly, when an individual shows you who they are by their words and actions, even in a joking manner, Believe them. That is WHO they are.

~ In Loving Memory of Diana Alejandra Keel

Author Sumorcon Little Harris

Sumorcon Little Harris

Sumorcon A. Little Harris is a woman after God's heart. She purposefully lives for the Glory of God; totally entrenched and deeply rooted in the work of God's Kingdom on so many levels. Her extraordinary vocal abilities bring a warm, anointed, spirit-filled sound of soul, empowerment and love to your ears and heart. As a teacher, she has an innate ability which clearly exudes love, truth and peace as she speaks Words of Wisdom from God that will honestly infuse and stir you deep within.

Sumorcon was born July 20, 1980 in Charlotte, North Carolina. At the age of five, she sparked an interest for singing and playing the piano, which all started in her grandmother's home. Never losing her passion for music as she grew, she took lessons in piano for five years and participated in school groups, church choirs, and served as a Praise & Worship Leader. Her vocal abilities also enable her to sing Quartet.

In 2007, she stepped out on faith to pursue a singing career in obedience to the vision God had placed within her. In November 2008, she held a Pre-Debut Celebration, which released her first CD project entitled: "To God Be the Glory" and in January 2014, she released her second CD entitled: "Alive in You". Both were well received and the release of her third CD project is scheduled for release in 2020. Sumorcon has and will perform for a wide range of occasions and social events; including engagements, weddings, church events and reunions. She specializes in Gospel, Smooth R& B and Smooth Jazz.

In 2014, she accepted the call to minister the Good News to all of God's children. She also started a non-profit organization entitled "Ministries Outside the 4 Walls". It's designed to meet the needs of the community; holding workshops and bible studies groups. In addition, she provides support, resources and guidance to many. She has brought church outside the four walls to connect with God's children in a way of real truth, where love is spoken, shown and lived.

Sumorcon serves as the Director of Legacy Empowerment Center and Afterschool Program for Legacy Ministries of Gastonia. Shepherded by the Holy Spirit of God, Sumorcon has become a woman who is God-fearing, humble and determined to run the race of life with integrity, vigor and purpose. She is a wife, mother of two young men, and a grandmother of one; each role she clearly views as a true blessing from God. It is her fervent prayer that God will ALWAYS keep her humble and surround her with positive people, and that in

EVEYTHING she does, GOD WILL FOREVER BE GLORIFIED.

Connect with Sumorcon Little-Harris
sumorcon.wixsite.com/voiceofspirit
sumorcon.wixsite.com/mot4walls

OVERCOMING THROUGH THE VOICE

I completely lost my state of being. Totally flat-lined. A tornado caught and swallowed me up in the wind. Holding me and not letting go of me. Taking me to the waters to die in the shallow parts of the ocean. Drowning me, never to see land again. As the water took me under, I closed my eyes to give up the ghost, but I heard this quiet voice say, "Fight". I replied, "What? Why? Why should I fight? Fight to live a life in which happiness will never be as long as he's alive. Fight to continue to receive his foolishness and disrespect, while listening to his theory of how *he's* the victim. He wants my life to be full of suffering and hell. So, no thank you! I'd rather give up the ghost."

However, the voice encouraged me not to give up but to trust Him. As His hand reached to save me, I fought against the voice that I heard because I did not want to be saved. It wasn't until I felt the gentle, yet powerful presence and touch of the voice that I was convinced that I would be safe in His arms. The voice whispered in my ear, "I got you. Trust me. I will turn your sorrows and pain into joy. I have plans for your life. Trust me." So, I stopped fighting the voice and gave the voice my hand saying, "Yes, God I will trust you".

The Story:

My life began to roll like a movie script. Rollercoaster scenes with inevitable ups and downs; good and bad plots dealing with high drama and poor choices. However, the most devastating part of my life was having dated the wrong man for five years; ignoring the signs, and then committing to marriage with him for five long years!

He was abusive, controlling, and manipulative. I met him at the age of 14. He was 19. I conceived my first child when I was 15 years old. Conceiving a child as a young teenager not only turned my life upside down but impacted those who surrounded me. Through all the pain and darkness I experienced, the sun truly did shine at the end. My son was born! I gave my life up to follow Jesus! My whole mind shifted; I changed! For me, the bars were now raised on my life; my child gave me purpose. People on the outside had their own negative opinions about how my life would end up since I was now a teenage mom. I was determined to prove them wrong. I concentrated on my education; striving to secure a good future for my child. As for the father of my child, he started to show me a different side of his personality. I thought he would support me and be proud of my accomplishments. He wasn't. I thought he'd be on board with proving the naysayers wrong by overcoming the challenges and breaking through the barriers. Barriers our son would not have to go through. I thought that together, we would demonstrate for our son, how to successfully play the games of life. I did not want our son struggling only to gain nothing in a life which can give you everything. But the father of my baby did not support my dream. His attitude, absence, inability to pick up the phone and call, and unapologetic cheating became the way of life for me. Being manipulative, he used jealously to control me. Eventually, he became verbally, mentally, emotionally and physically abusive.

I turned down two full-ride college scholarships that included childcare and housing support just because he said, "Why you want to do that? You can't make it in another city by yourself with a baby. I'm not going to be driving up there to see you two. Well, we might need to call it quits now!" When he said that, it was like someone grabbed my heart and crushed the life out of it. He declared, "You have to choose me or school. Nobody will want you. Nobody is going to want to deal with some girl with a baby. You're ruining your life!" Young and naïve, I chose him. Love blinded me to the fact that this was a man who was insecure, suffered from low self-esteem and had experienced hurt. As a result, he put on a good front, but was driven by bitterness and jealousy. I let this evil man convince me to give up my opportunity to go to college! He knew once I left for college, I was going to better my life for me and my son. I had an opportunity full of possibilities. Life provided me hope and a chance to win. But I didn't choose it. I should have been wise. Wise enough not to allow the negative words of a man stop me from achieving. You don't know how many times I blame myself for not taking those scholarships. Life could have been so different. I had enough for the both of us. Over time, my anger grew and multiplied over the ramifications of this one poor choice. It took a long time to heal, forgive and release that moment in time from my mental space.

I gave up college and stayed with this man. Fully committing, I later married this man. Looking back, I now know that I gave him too much of me. Unselfishly, I gave him my love, honesty, time, money and so much more. While, in return, he gave me heartache, excuses, loneliness, lies, broken promises and bruises. There are many kinds of abuse. I believe I just might have experienced the majority, if not all of them. I experienced verbal, emotional, mental, physical and economic abuse. While experiencing all of these, I sat in silence. I didn't speak a word to anyone because he was becoming a minister at our home church. I didn't want his reputation to be discredited. Yet, shaking my head, I discredited myself and diminished my self- worth to elevate him. Now, as I think over it, I needed to have put him on the front-page news! I should have let the whole world know who he really was. The man I knew him to be.

When I gave birth to my second son, this man wasn't even there. He only showed up on the scene when we were required to make a church appearance. It was like my whole life and my marriage were built on a lie. I have been slapped, punched, kicked and choked by this man who said he would love and protect me. I had been punched so hard that I blacked out and saw stars. I had temporary hearing lost in my left ear. There were numerous trips to the ER because he had kicked me so hard between my legs that treatment was required. I had been left with bruises that I tried to cover up with makeup. But I wasn't a makeup girl. I often wondered if anyone noticed the discoloration of my face.

My car had broken down on the side of the road multiple times and yet, he never came to see about me. Not even when our boys were with me. We had to walk in the bitter winter air, to the closest exit. Just because he wouldn't answer the phone. His brother came and picked me and my babies up and took us home. When we arrived, he was there. His brother became angry with him. He really let him have it. You know what happened next. Once his brother left, he started to argue and fight with me. To hear my 7-month-old baby crying to the top of his lungs and my 7-year-old screaming "Daddy, please stop and leave Mommie alone", really sparked something in me. Our son said, "I promise you I will be a good boy. Just leave Mommie alone". That broke me down. At that moment, I knew this was affecting my babies. Unfortunately, that was the first of many occasions. My children would witness many more acts of abuse. I tried everything possible to get this man to stop and get right. I can give you a penny for every time I heard- "I am sorry, I won't do it again" or "Don't leave me, I love you". However, it became a broken record on repeat. I faced a lot throughout the marriage. However, the worst was that it was at the cost of my children's wellbeing.

I still have insecurities and I am healing. He repeatedly told me, "Everything is your fault. You're fat; disgusting to look at. The boys will never respect nor love you because you're weak". Yes, his verbal abuse still effects my self-esteem today. He said I wasn't good enough to be kept. To hear something like that! Those statements cut inside out leaving me to bleed to death. The sad part is, I believed it. I allowed the words of a monster, who was jealous of the relationship I had with my sons, to damage me. Yes, it's been 15 years since I've been divorced but it's a process. After the divorce, I thought the hurt and pain would be over.

Nope! Not at all. When you think you've been dragged so low, you wonder how much lower you can go.

Well, he took me to court and was awarded custody of our oldest son. After all he'd done to our family! He had the audacity to pretend he was a man of moral standards and used the fact that he was a preacher to serve as evidence. I can't provide words to describe how I felt. I'm just now releasing the anger and rage I carried which was destroying me. So, I had to forgive. I sought it for myself. Yes, I had to give myself permission to let go so I could heal. Economically, I carried the household. I was married on paper but single as it related to responsibilities. Till this day, I don't know how his full income was spent. It sure wasn't spent to support the home. I do know that some of it was spent on maintaining his image. This man was flashy; he had to be the center of attention. He styled in Stacy Adams attire with bling around his neck and on his fingers. While, my children and I were trying to just survive. We didn't look the part of the preacher's wife and sons. We did not look like we belonged to him. I had to keep a roof over our heads, purchase food for my boys to eat and cover daycare cost for the baby boy. Many days, we were without. But he was living large and having affairs with other women. Of course, he came up with so many excuses as to why he couldn't help with the bills. He used isolation as a control technique. I wasn't allowed to have a cell phone, connect with my friends, be around my family or work to achieve any of my personal goals. I was only permitted to sing in the church choir. I had had dreams of becoming a singer. He completely obliterated that dream. Yes, he had complete control of me and every move I made.

He moved us around Charlotte so many times that before I left him, my oldest son had gone to eight different elementary schools. Due to the abuse, my oldest son began acting out, both at home and at school. Imitating his dad, he caused many scenes at school. My son had witnessed the abuse that his father poured out on me. Now there were times when he, himself experienced abuse. No child should be disciplined by being forced to lay across a bed with no clothes on and dared not to move. Whipped with a belt. Not some average belt. Many times, for something that could have been handled another way.

I was sick and tired of the abuse, infidelity and the fake image of a marriage. I summoned the courage and left him. He played the victim and went out and told everybody that I had walked out on him. I, on the other hand, kept silent. Our separation caused chaos in the church and there were demands from many of the members for us to reconcile. After a month or two, I was convinced to go back to him. However, things never changed. Once again, everything went back to the way it was before the separation. Again, there were many broken promises. Once again, I was back taking care of all the finances and being a prisoner in my own home. Until one day, he disappeared from us and didn't return home until early the next morning. He had left us home with nothing to eat or drink. I had no money and there was no gas in my car. I questioned him about where he had been all day which led to a heated argument and fighting. It just so happened that our pastors came by because they felt that something was wrong. The man punched me in front of our pastors! Something clicked and I fought back!

As he was choking me, I began giving up on life. But that's also when the voice spoke, telling me not to give up. I was done! I packed up my stuff and my babies and left for the last time! I was a shipwreck: crashing against the rocks. A toy spinning top; spinning out of control. Yet, I had to move forward. I rented an apartment. And now I was on the path of *a new beginning.* Once I broke my silence, I can't tell you how many times I heard "I thought something was going on". All I did was smile; "like really."

REFLECTIONS OF AN OVERCOMER:

1.) Never allow yourself to give up on your dreams, opportunities or desires that help your life to expand and grow into the full empire that you deserve. Do not allow someone who is selfish and does not have your best interest at heart to distract or discourage you. If someone supports and loves you, they'll be there for you; cheering you on every step of the way. Believe in yourself enough. Enough to conquer the world; not allowing the voices of the haters or nay-sayers to negatively impact your life

2.) Abuse affects the innocents. Children will act out due to the atmosphere and circumstances that surround them. We as parents, should never allow our children to be put into situations where their lives are negatively altered. Nor should they have to choose between parents. Remember, children see and hear everything, even if you think they don't know what is happening. They are much smarter than we give them credit for.

3.) As we're faced with this ugly case of abuse, we must remember who we are. No matter what someone says or how they make you feel, never ever forget who God created you to be. We are jewels that will shine. If you are in this situation or witness to an abusive situation, I encourage you to fight! Keep your faith because I tell you, God will never let you fall. I kept my faith and focus in and on God. I had to fight not just for myself but for my sons. Also, for you. To let someone know you are not alone. Yes, we may have been victims, but we are now overcomers. God allowed our pain to be a testimony to others to share and heal the brokenness. As the process begins, I encourage you to get your life back and live each day greater than the day before. Many victims didn't make it. Their lives we'll remember but we're here to sound the alarm. I believe, we are destined to be on this earth to do something incredible in their honor and to share our story.

4.) I can't express it enough. Abuse is more than physical. It can take many forms. It can be sexual, verbal, emotional, economic or more. All forms work on our mental state of being. So, recognize the signs. If there's someone who's in an abusive situation, I promise you that there is life afterwards. I left that man and took back control of my life. Three years after the divorce I released my first gospel album. My third album will be released 2020. It was like a dream come true! Being on stage, singing and spreading the "Good News". I'm the CEO of Ministries Outside the 4 Walls. An organization that services the community in various ways. We minister outside the church to the community to build or rebuild relationships based on trust. By being understanding and just ourselves. No titles or falsehoods. Just genuine, authentic relationships without judgement. Eleven years after the marriage was over, I met and married a man who was like my knight in shining armor! When I tell you! My husband now, loves me in ways I'd never experienced before. My sons and I have relationships that are healthy, harmonious and ongoing. After their father tried to destroy our bond, it backfired. God shifted things around for the greater good. I had to be kind and patient with myself. In addition, I had to forgive him and myself. Ask for forgiveness. As hard as it was; it was a must do for my sanity.

Listen, you are not by yourself. Chose to fight because God always has a plan for you! A joy for your morning. It's not what you've been through but it's how you go through it. Be encouraged my brothers and sisters. We are OVERCOMERS!

Author Keekee Lennay

Author Keekee Lennay

Keekee Lennay, is an overcomer and race winner! Originally from Detroit, Michigan, Keekee currently resides in the Raleigh, North Carolina area. Keekee is a Health and Confidence Coach who uses her life experiences to inspire and empower others.

After leaving a toxic relationship and overcoming domestic violence, Keekee decided to take control of her life and her health. Keekee worked hard and was successful in losing over 80 pounds. Keekee ran a half marathon and started implementing small changes to her lifestyle to become healthier and happier.

Keekee strives to show women that living a healthy lifestyle can be made simple and on their terms. She coaches girls to tap into their authentic self and love the body they live in. Keekee also coaches women to heal and find "life after" a traumatic experience. She wants women to know that their life can be fulfilling and magical again. When she is not coaching and empowering others, Keekee loves to dance, and enjoy good music, good vibes and Beyoncé!

Keekee Lennay

Connect with Keekee Lennay:
FB:Keekee Lennay
Instagram:@ keekeelennay
Remember in ALL things be YOU!

OVERCOMING HIS BELITTLING SPIRIT

I saw him give a girl his number.... I was 20 minutes early for meeting him. I thought it would be a surprise. I worked through my lunch to surprise him because I felt bad that I would be a few minutes late to a party he was so excited about. We had just spent my birthday weekend together, and it was one of the best weekends EVER, and I had just uttered the three words that ignites any relationship: "I love you." He told me first, however, I had been scared to say it back; but after the weekend we just had I had no choice but to express those feelings because there was no doubt in my mind that what I felt was real. So, there was no way I could be late. I had to show up. I had to be on his arm. This man that I loved. This man that every time I looked at him; he made my heart smile. This man that claimed his crew was excited to finally meet me. I had to be on time.

I walked in smiling so hard from ear to ear. Excited to see his expression, but what I saw stopped me dead in my tracks. My immediate thought was, "maybe they are just connecting on Facebook; that has to be it, that's innocent. That's the world we live in now". Then I heard her say, "I can't wait to hang out next weekend, call me this week to set it up." My thoughts immediately went to how I was supposed to be out of town next weekend. I froze. What does she mean, she can't wait to hang out next weekend and why do they have to hang out on the one weekend I won't be in town? I waited until the girl walked away. I walked up and yea, he was surprised alright. I asked him what that was about, and his reply was "we were connecting on social media" Damn, he knew me so well. My response was, "Oh, okay well it sounds like you all have plans next weekend; maybe that should wait until I'm here and we can all hang out together."

Shit. Hit. The. Fan!

He grabbed my arm so tight. Not aggressive enough to where people around us could see, but tight enough that I was uncomfortable. He pulled me close and whispered, "We aren't going to start this jealousy thing, I love you, you know that. You're not the weak, jealous type; that's what I love about you most. You're stronger than that" Then, he grabbed and pinched my arm and kissed me on the forehead and said let's dance.

I should have run then, but I went to the dance floor and danced, like no one was watching. He was right. I am strong. I am not the jealous type. He loves me and I finally admitted that I loved him. He is allowed to have female friends. It didn't matter that their plans were made on a weekend I wouldn't be in town. That had to have been a coincidence. So we danced. Danced the problem away. Looking back, that was the first in-your-face red flag and I completely ignored it. I danced.

Growing up I never saw anything close to any form of abuse. Like any family, we had our issues, our secrets, and our drama, but domestic violence? Never saw anything that resembled it. So, when I was asked why I didn't walk away when I saw the first red flag, I answered honestly by saying "I didn't know it was a red flag". I moved to Raleigh, North Carolina with my parents and siblings and it was one of the best decisions I have ever made. I have zero regrets regarding the move; however, no one warns you that, as an adult, it's not so easy to meet new people and make new friends. So, when this man and I met and connected on a few interests, it was a breath of fresh air. I remember thinking- "FINALLY". We started to hang out as just friends, but I hold all men to the same standards, no matter the association.

While he was just my friend, he made me feel safe in our new relationship. So, when he asked me to be his girlfriend, there was no hesitation; the answer was "YES!" He didn't have much and had been open and honest about his past as a convicted felon, but what he had, he gave to me freely and that was enough for me. When my parents came to me and told me they would be moving to Georgia and asked if I wanted to take another move with them, I confidently answered- "NO", because, for the first time since living in North Carolina, I felt safe, secure, and comfortable. I didn't want to leave my newfound love. I was watching my mom leave her driveway and head to the highway for Georgia; had I known what my life would be like for the next two and a half years, I would have chased her down and jumped in the car.

Like I previously said, I had no idea what domestic abuse looked like. I hadn't grown up around it; no one close to me had ever shared a story, and what little I knew about domestic abuse came from my binge watching of Law & Order SVU. So when my boyfriend started making statements like "Kee you really are average in the looks department, but I love you anyway, so it's okay." or "I don't normally date girls your size, but I made an exception for you." and "You need to tell me where you are at all times and what you're doing, that's how you show me you respect me." I didn't realize that those are forms of emotional abuse, which is a part of domestic abuse. I could go on and on about the belittling things he said that he "softened" by saying something positive, yet condescending on the end of his jabs. Just know that he had a way of saying the most hurtful things and ending them with an - "I love you so much," that I never recognized the signs.

After the incident at the party, everything went back to normal, so I assumed his behavior, that night, was a one-time thing. I convinced myself that, because I didn't have a bruise on my arm, the "pinch and grab" really didn't hurt and I was over-exaggerating things in my head. I was proven wrong when that crazy temper of his reared its ugly head. Once again. I got a promotion at my job and we had plans to celebrate. I came home from work, and when I walked through the door, I could tell someone other than my boyfriend had been in our home. I shook that crazy thought off and said to myself, "It's his home too, he can have company here. Chill out, sis. You're being possessive and territorial."

The apartment we lived in was in my name, due to his record, and he often expressed that it seemed that I felt like he lived with me, instead of this being our home together. To avoid him feeling this way, I checked my intuition because the apartment was indeed ours. I got dressed and "Slayed to the Gawds". My hair was on point, pedicure still fresh, so peep toe pumps were a must, and even with the weight gain I was starting to experience, I still wore a dress that literally turned heads. Getting dressed up like that wasn't my norm nor my favorite vibe, but he loved it and that was enough for me. I was also excited to celebrate with him and to see his face when he saw me dressed. Like any traditional night on the town, it started with "pre-game" drinks before heading downtown. I wasn't a drinker, so he pretty much was drinking by himself, but he was in a good mood and I was feeling his playful banter. I knew the alcohol played a role in his carefree attitude, so when I saw the potential spiral that could happen flash before my eyes, I brushed it off because we were in for a night to remember.

When we got downtown, he couldn't get into any bars or restaurants because he left his ID at home and they could smell the E&J on his breath. This frustrated him and he became irritable. I tried to take control of the situation by flirting and saying, "we could have more fun at home any way," giving him a look that would make most men run to take me home but E&J had won and my man didn't like what I said. He began to cause a scene in the middle of downtown Raleigh, saying I was against him and I always took everyone's side except his. He forgot his ID at home, bouncers wouldn't let him in because of that. I understood; I have no clue why he did not. He felt that I wasn't an ally and therefore, I deserved to be cursed out in the middle of Glenwood Avenue and that's exactly what he did. I was also told that my dress was ugly and I didn't look good on his arm, so he couldn't convince the bouncer to let us in because I didn't "look the part". Somehow a night that was supposed to be a night of fun and celebration turned into a night of me questioning my loyalty to him, feeling like I wasn't pretty enough, and vowing to never touch alcohol if it made me turn into the type of person he became that night. His words cut deep and they were harsh. I had never heard so many "ugly and stupid bitches" thrown at someone in the way he threw those words at me. I was shocked, baffled, and embarrassed. All I wanted to do was go home and end that night. When we got home, he wanted to cash in on the look I gave him earlier. I wasn't in the mood, I was turned off and my feelings were hurt, but he had been turned away enough that night and I wasn't going to do the same to him; so, I obliged. I blamed E&J for his behavior and convinced myself that it wasn't really him talking to me the way he did; it was the alcohol. If I could get him to leave the alcohol alone, then our relationship would be perfect. It was no way this was abuse in any form; alcohol was the issue and I vowed to eliminate it so my relationship wouldn't suffer. I quickly learned I was wrong. Alcohol wasn't the issue; he was.

The lying and cheating was starting to become the norm. I had become numb to it and whenever I confronted him he would push me into the nearest wall. I prayed a prayer every night that stated- "Thank you God for stopping him from bruising my face." I knew if that ever happened, there was no way I could hide what was going on in our home. At this point, I discovered that I was pregnant with his child. I made the ultimate decision that I would not bring an innocent child into our toxic mess; especially when there were rumors of him having fathered another child. I couldn't believe I made that decision, but I knew I had no business being with him, and I definitely wasn't going to force my child to deal with him. I handled the situation the best way I knew how. While it was my choice, I still dealt with that painful loss daily.

He had lost his job and I was financially carrying the relationship. It was becoming stressful and like many people, I dealt with the stress and the strain of it all with food. I started gaining weight and it only made matters worse. I caught him cheating, yet again, and he blamed my weight gain for his infidelity. He told me he had sex with other women because he was no longer attracted to me. I felt low, ugly and unworthy, and while feeling all those emotions, I found the strength to call him a *coward.* I guess me calling him exactly what he was hit a different kind of nerve, because he finally did it. He punched me dead in the face causing a busted lip, broken eye glasses, and pain like I had never felt before. I felt defeated.

After being punched in the face I was completely checked out of the relationship. He continued to lie, cheat, manipulate, and say mean and hurtful things, but I got to the point where I wanted out so badly that I didn't even care. I knew I only had to make one phone call to my parents and I would be fine, but to be truly honest, I was so embarrassed that I didn't even know how to make that call. I was what I thought was a strong woman, but I had let a man put his hands on me and that made me feel weak. We got into a big argument and this time I fought back. It shocked him but, I also think I scared him. So, instead of making matters worse, he left the house to cool off. I took my chance and headed to Charlotte for a business training and that began my process of overcoming.

He got home and was shocked that I wasn't there. He called me a million times while I was away. I wasn't interested in hearing what he had to say and for the first time in a long time, I felt safe. I was with a group of people who, while I tried my best to stay distant from them, they worked even harder to keep me on their check-in radar. I gave in to his calls and almost gave in to his plea for forgiveness until I heard a friend say, "HANG UP THE PHONE NOW! You don't have to deal with that now, I'm here, you're okay." Those words gave me strength. It was someone else's belief in me that made me understand the power I had to walk away. To hear, "You're okay!" was music to my ears because, if I am being honest, I didn't think I would be okay without him. I still thank that person often because those words changed my life. Anytime I doubted myself, I would repeat to myself, "You're okay." I had had enough, and I wasn't going to be the victim anymore. That strength came from loving myself enough to do whatever it took to get him out of my home. I had to dig deep to love Kee enough to not endure pain and misery. I had to search for a love within myself that surprisingly was tough to find, to no longer accept love in a way that hurt. I made a choice and I chose me.

Confidently and boldly, I told my abuser he was no longer welcomed in my house and he needed to leave. He tried to fight me, but what he saw in my eyes was no longer fear and that is when I took my power back. He no longer controlled my thoughts and feelings about myself. I started taking my health seriously and started to lose weight and make better choices. While he was the reason I got on the scale, what I saw disgusted me and I needed to make a change fast. I began to fall in love with Kee and did that by taking care of my temple. He tried to bruise my body, I decided to love it and doing that made me see my worth.

Love for Kee became all the strength I needed; and I vowed to never stop loving myself ever again. I am an OVERCOMER!

REFLECTIONS OF AN OVERCOMER:

1. **Not being aware of the red flag.** So many women just aren't aware that something is wrong. They think it's a one-time incident until the one-time incidents keep repeating themselves.

2. **Giving in to sex**----I did this soooooo many times. Playing by the rule of- *if he doesn't get it from me, he will get it elsewhere,* so I should give my MAN what he wants-----this should NEVER be the case.

3. **Thinking that because he hadn't bruised me it was abuse**----just because you don't have visible scars doesn't mean you aren't scarred.

4. **Making tough calls----**I never thought I would be the girl who would have an abortion but in that moment, it was the decision I knew I had to make.

5. **Learning to love my body saved my life**----it was that love that gave me strength to leave.

Author

Susan Groce Newnam

Susan Gorce Newnam

Susan Newnam is a true Overcomer! As the daughter of a Federal employee, Susan lived in six different states by the time she was a teenager. Of all her places of residency, Susan is most proud to call North Carolina her home, for the last 30 years.

Susan has had a successful career in sales, but her true JOY comes from helping others. Susan has been happily married, for the last 10 years, and has three beautiful children. She hopes that her written words, and the other powerful stories shared in this book, will find their way to those that need to read them the most. There is no reason for us to live in silence.

Contact Susan:
Color street stylists www.colorstreet.com/susannewnam

OVERCOMING THE MANIPULATION

I got married when I was 22. He was 29. I met him in a bar. He was a bouncer, and he was cute. He walked my friends and me from my car into the building, kept an eye on us throughout the night, and I was sure to flirt with him anytime he was close. He asked me to dance with him on the last song, and my heart was all fluttery. I couldn't believe he wanted anything to do with me, but he did. We exchanged numbers, talked on the phone a lot, went on a few dates, all the normal things that couples who are dating do. He went to church with me, which was very important to me, and to my family. He was baptized. "Wow! This might be going somewhere!" I thought. Within eight months of meeting, he proposed. We went to marriage counseling. He was considerate, respectful, caring, attentive, loving, and a wolf in sheep's clothing. We got into an argument on our honeymoon, about something insignificant, which I chalked up to us being tired, because after all, he loved me… right? When we got home, he threatened to divorce me because I used my maiden name as my middle name when I got my new driver's license. I was so dumbfounded that he would be so upset over something so small. I didn't know I needed his *permission* to choose my name. Isn't that the way everyone did it? The arguments were frequent, and usually because I didn't so something the way he wanted. Each one broke my self- esteem a little more. Most of them ended up with me pined up against the wall with his hands around my throat. He would hold me there and scream in my face that I was stupid, and a child, and that he never should have married me! How could he say he loved me and then treat me like this? Other arguments would include him shoving me into furniture, or across the bed leaving bruises on my legs or arms, but not really any that I could "prove" he caused, but each one leaving me feeling less and less worthy of being loved, but also angrier and angrier that I thought he was "the one", and that I had been taken advantage of.

I am a redhead. The redhead temper is real. I don't like to be told what to do, or how to do it. I don't deny that I could have backed down from whatever we were fighting about at any time, and possibly prevented the "push and shove", but that wasn't me. It still isn't. It won't ever be.

We were married for 11 months, and after leaving him for three weeks, I returned home to give it one last try. I was strong, and that's what strong women do; they fight for what they believe in. They finish what they start. The third night home, I wasn't in the mood for sex. That is not what he wanted to hear. He started yelling at me and calling me names, so I got up and went to the bedroom down the hall. He followed. Yelling. Cursing. Threatening. His fists were clenched. I threw a chair at him to slow him down, but he caught it and threw it aside and went into the living room. I put my shoes on and decided that I was DONE. I knew that this was not the kind of marriage God wanted for me. I knew that my husband did not love me the way Christ loves his church. I knew that I could not live like that. And I knew that I wasn't being strong WITH him, I was being a coward for not owning up to the mistake of choosing the wrong man. It was time to face the embarrassment of divorce. It was time to face the disgrace of a broken marriage.

I went into the living room to get my purse and keys, and he said, "Where do you think you are going?" I said "I'm leaving. This time for good." He said "I will beat the Sh!t out of you before you leave!" Cue-*redhead temper.* I got right up in his face and said "You know, Mother Fuc$er.. you go ahead and make it count this time! You be sure to leave a BIG bruise!" Then he cold cocked me. Right in the nose. HARD. I went down. But I got back up as he broke our wedding photo over the coffee table and shoved me into the glass saying, "THIS is our marriage!" He came at me again and I dug my nails into his bare chest to hold him off. We ended up in the kitchen where he shoved me again onto the floor. He grabbed the back of my hair and held me down on the floor punching me continuously in the chest yelling at me to move my hands when I tried to shield myself from the blows. We had been fighting for a few hours when he got in my face and threatened to kill me. And my parents. And my sisters. And their boyfriends if they got in his way. I knew that there was no way I was leaving that night. Time to switch gears and put my game face on. As tears streamed down my face, I convinced him that I was sorry. I convinced him that I would stay with him forever. I convinced him that I agreed with his theory that my parents controlled me and were even abusive to me as a child. I convinced him that I would never speak to them again.

As we "kissed and made up", I remembered a domestic case my dad had worked on during his many years in law enforcement. The case involved the sweetest couple I had ever met, who were new to our church family. I remembered seeing pictures of her swollen eyes. Pictures of her bruised face, arms, and neck. I remembered hearing the words "Arrest, Restraining Order, Proof". I also remembered seeing a bag of her hair on the table. I remembered how no one could believe that this had happened to her. No one could believe that her sweet husband was the one who had done it to her. PROOF. I finally had my PROOF. We went back to bed, and I pretended to be asleep. Our house was filled with guns, and he kept one on the headboard of our waterbed. It took everything in me not to use it on him that night. The only thing that stopped me was fear. Fear that he would turn it on me instead, and carry out his threat to do the same to my family. He eventually got up and went into the living room and watched TV. All Night.

The next morning when I got up to get ready for work, he was still in the living room. Terrified that he would see through my lies, and angry for how he had fooled me, I got in the shower. As I washed my hair, handfuls would come out. Remembering the bag of hair, I stuck them all on the shower wall. I got dressed for work, without make-up, and put the hair from the shower wall in a baggie in my jacket pocket. Before I left, he made sure to point out the claw marks on his chest where I had tried to push him away, and how I had hurt him. It was then that I knew I had to do something. I had to make sure I never had to go back to that house ever again. I kissed him goodbye and told him I would see him after work.

I drove to work as fast as I could. I worked with my mom, and as soon as she saw me, she burst into tears, crying out- "Oh my God! What did he do to you?" We called my dad and he came and took me to the Sheriff's Department to file an emergency restraining order, as well as every police station in town to show his picture. I remember sitting in that courtroom, waiting for my case to be heard, and listening to the male judge practically berate the poor woman in front of me because the only "PROOF" she has was a bruise on her wrist where her husband grabbed her in a drunken rage. I remember how sad I felt for her that she was most likely going to have to go back home to her abuser. I was worried that I wasn't going to have enough "PROOF" to get my own protective order. As my request was granted, I then felt saddened that the level of abuse that I had endured the night before is what it would take for other women to be protected as well. The time, 5:00 pm came and went, and I didn't go home after work. He started calling me. Over and over. He called my parents' house acting all sweet asking my mom if I had mentioned stopping somewhere before I went home. He said he was worried. My dad took the phone from my mom and told him he had better be worried. "She's not coming home. Not tonight. Not ever!"

Now we waited. For the police to arrest him. Friends and family would call to check on me as they heard the news. The phone would ring. My stomach would drop. Not the police. The phone would ring again. My stomach would drop harder. Not the police. At one point I stood up and started screaming- "IF YOU AREN'T THE POLICE DON'T CALL!!" I wanted to get out of the house, so I didn't have to hear any more of the talk about what had happened. I wanted to take a walk around the block. Dad said- "No, I can't protect you out there". The call finally came around 9:00 pm to inform us of his arrest. We took five vehicles to the house to get all of my belongings. When we got there the door from the carport to the kitchen was locked and dead-bolted. MY

KEY DIDN'T FIT! I lost it in the driveway, screaming that the police took so long to arrest him that he had time to change the locks. I was so angry that I took a tire iron and busted the glass out of the basement door and went through the house and unlocked the front door for everyone and "invited them in" to get my things. We only took the necessities and left the heavy stuff. I had just had a huge Tupperware party and my mom wanted to dump everything out of all of it onto the floor and take the Tupperware with us! We actually laughed for a minute but decided against it.

He spent one night in jail. ONE NIGHT. Just enough to make him angrier than he already was. He made threatening calls to my parents' house. He made accusations that we stole his property. He threatened to have my dad arrested for breaking and entering. None of it worked. 10 days later, the courts granted my request for a 365-day restraining order. six weeks later, I was escorted back to the house to gather the rest of my belongings, and the two officers were more interested in the latest hunting "trophy" he had killed, than they were about what I needed.

In the state we lived in, there has to be a separation period of one year and one day before divorce proceedings can begin. We had only been married for 11 months, so we were going to have to be separated longer than we were married! I get it on some level. You made a commitment. You honor your commitment. Till death do you part. A year should give you plenty of time to think about ending that commitment or not. But it can also force someone in my position to have to go back. To a dangerous situation. To the possible death that will part them. I was very fortunate to have family that was close by. Family that wanted the best for me. To protect me. It kept me from ever thinking about going back. I never saw him again.

During the year that I was separated, I met someone else. He was new to the area and went to our church. He came to my parents' house for dinner a few times. He came to some of my softball games. We sat together at church potlucks and became friends. During a phone conversation, I was telling him what I had recently been through, and that it was my belief that I would never be able to marry again because God hates divorce. I wasn't divorcing my husband because he cheated on me, I was divorcing him because he was physically abusive. I told him that I would rather be alone for the rest of my life, than to be that man's wife! He replied: "That's too bad, because I was hoping one day you could be MY wife." Those words sparked something in me. Someone else actually WANTED me to be their wife. How could I just settle for being single?

It wasn't long before I allowed him to take me out on dates. We got to know each other better. He was 38. I was 24. But I had been through things that most 24-year olds can't even imagine. He shared his rough childhood with me. I felt sorry for him. I wanted to make life better for him; happier for him. Then the worst best thing happened. I was pregnant. My divorce was still several months from being final. My loving, supportive parents were devastated. Our friends and church family turned their backs on us. How were we possibly going to do this? But we pushed through.

One week after my divorce was final, we got married in a small ceremony in my parents' back yard. Two months later, we welcomed a son. My new husband had recently changed jobs and moved in with us at my parents' house until we could get on our feet. We were there for two years. During that time, he was fired from no less than three jobs. He constantly stressed about money. He always had an excuse for not spending time with his son. He always had an excuse for losing the job.

I knew we could not live with my parents forever. So, I got a job. We moved into our own place. Over the next six years we would move three more times, have a beautiful baby girl, and he would lose or walk out on at least eight jobs. I would go through four jobs, each one with a higher salary than the last, and parting on good terms, but we were always low on money. We were always fighting. He always worked jobs that kept him out late at night. He always slept late. Housework was *my* job. Grocery shopping was *my* job. Hot meals waiting for him at midnight were expected, even though I had to be up with the kids early enough to get them to school and daycare while I worked. If I ever had to stay at work longer than normal, he would accuse me of having an affair, or doing something I wasn't supposed to be doing. If I didn't "check in" at a designated time, or answer his call no matter what, I was having an affair. If my male boss would call me about concerns specific to the job, I was having an affair. I was living in defense all the time.

He never hit me. But sometimes I wished he would. Sometimes, I felt like I would better understand his feelings towards me if he did. But the WORDS. The WORDS hurt so much more than the blow to the face that took me down all those years ago. How was I back here? How did I allow this to happen again? How could I be so naive? How could I be so

STUPID? There it is. STUPID. The word that hurt the most. The one he used the most.

It didn't take long for me to understand why he couldn't keep a job. He was a good employee. While he was good with customers or clients, he was TERRIBLE to the staff. They feared him. They hated him. They had zero respect for him. Eventually, the person in charge of him would recognize it and let him go. His kids recognized it, too. Our son tried so hard to get his father to spend time with him. "Daddy, will you come eat lunch with me at school sometime?", to which he would reply, "Why would I want to do that? School lunches are gross!" "Daddy will you take me to the movies this weekend?" "Kids' movies are stupid. I don't have time for that." It was never ending. Our daughter was terrified of him. She was terrified of most men. She would hit people that would get too close. She would bite people that got even closer. She would get in trouble at daycare. We had a sweet lady that offered to keep her, and it worked well for a time. However, she started running away and fighting me when I would pick her up at the end of the day. She didn't want to go home! She was also allowed to do whatever she wanted at the babysitter's house, as long as she didn't get hurt, but knew she had to follow the rules at home. I made the decision to leave my job and open a Home-Daycare. That was the only way to be able to stay home with my kids, take care of the house, and still create an income. My husband's late-night dinner demands made it hard to be ready for children to start arriving at 6 AM. His "keep those kids quiet while I sleep till noon" demands made it even harder. But being home with my kids allowed me to be there for them in ways that he refused.

I felt like a fool. I felt like a failure. I felt unworthy of true love. I had failed at marriage. Again. I was failing my children, who had no idea what it meant to be loved by their father. The sadness on my son's face when his father would be too busy sleeping, to spend time with him, was heartbreaking. The fear on his face when his father would yell at him for being too loud was maddening. The fact that our daughter would cringe away from him if he got close to her was too much to witness. I was a big girl, and he could say whatever he wanted to hurt me, but he was not going to hurt my kids. Not anymore. At one point, I even considered calling my first husband and convincing him to help me "take care of him". That was clearly my lowest point, and I knew that I had to end the cycle.

I told him how I felt. I told him to move out. I gave him 30 days. I was no longer asking for anything. I was no longer concerned with his feelings. I had to make a better life for my children, even if I had to do it alone. Maybe alone was better. He tried to convince me to give us another chance. He tried to convince me to have another baby. He promised to be the most loving and devoted husband and father ever. It was tempting. But it wouldn't have lasted. I could not risk one more minute of happiness on his empty promises.

The 12 years that would follow would be some of the best worst days of my life! They were the best days because I was FREE. Because I had a friend. A best friend. A best friend who would later become my husband. A husband that loves me the way Christ loves his church. A husband who loves my children like they are his own. A husband whom my children love as if he was there father.

My ex-husband HATED my new husband. He claimed that he "stole his family" and did everything he could to spread lies about us. Visitation was usually a struggle between me and the kids trying to convince them that they HAD to go, even though they didn't want to. Our daughter was only four years old and she would get as far away from him as possible, screaming at him, "I hate you! I'm not going anywhere with you! Don't touch me! I wish you weren't my dad!" Our son was nine and stood in front of him the same day and said, "We aren't going, and you can't make us!" so his father grabbed him by the back of the neck and shoved him into his car. I called the police and they made them go with him. When we picked them back up on Sunday afternoon, the kids ran to both of us, crying, and as my ex turned to get back in the car, he "flipped us the bird". Our son saw it, and when he told his father as much the next time he saw him. His father's response was, "I'm sorry you had to see that." No apology, ever. For anything. There were times where he would have a "bad weekend" with the kids and would come up with an excuse not to take them for his next visit and go for months without even contacting them. Those were good months for us, until he would want to see them, out of the blue and accuse me of trying to keep his kids from him if we had already made plans.

He even took us to court and accused me of trying to replace him with my new husband. The judge asked us if the kids were involved in any extra-curricular sports, and while pointing to my ex, I said "No, because heaven forbid these two be in the same space at the same time, because he can't handle it." The judge looked at me and said, "HE is their father, HE is not!" while pointing at the two men. I responded "Ma'am, with all due respect, DNA and a garnished paycheck does NOT make someone a FATHER!" My red-headed temper had gotten the best of me, again, and she actually gave my ex the *authority* to dictate where in public my husband could be if he was going to be there, too! Are you serious? I was pregnant with my third child and she actually threatened to put me in jail if I went against his wishes.

A few months later our daughter had a gymnastics recital, and my ex "allowed" my husband to come, but only because our daughter told him she would never talk to him again or ever respect him if he didn't. Then Mothers' Day came. All the years we were married he NEVER got me anything for Mother's Day. "You're not *my* mother", he would say. But this year he took the kids to get me a few things. They told him there was no need because my husband had already taken them. He insisted. He made sure he was the one to give me the gifts. I refused them, because it wasn't something he had ever done in the past, and it certainly wasn't his job anymore, and he was livid! The next thing I knew, we were hit with papers to appear in court again. This time he was suing for custody! I hired the meanest lawyer I could find, and when she was finished, the judge actually apologized to me! She told my ex that her decision to allow him to determine whether or not my husband could be in the same places as he was when the kids were present was not for him to have "a big stick to wave around, but to ease their way into some kind of co-existence".

There have been so many struggles. So many fights over visitation. So many arguments. So many trips to court because he wasn't getting his way. So many times, that I have felt my stomach drop the same way it did for all those years when the phone would ring, and his name would appear on the caller ID. But time. Time allows wounds to heal, and emotions to settle. It allows for self-esteem to rebuild. It also allows for courage to grow. When my son was about 13, he finally stood up to his dad. He told him that he didn't like the person he was and that he saw through the façade of the "loving father" he pretended to be. He also told him that he was not going with him for his scheduled weekend, and that his sister would not be coming either. He responded with "Well, I have a court order that says that you don't have a choice." My son said, "What are you going to do? Call the police? Mom isn't the one that says I'm not going, I am. So, go ahead and call them if you want. I would be happy to tell them why I don't want to go." My ex got in his car and made a phone call and my son stood his ground. My ex actually called a friend who advised him to let it go and not force the issue, but even though we thought he was calling the police, my son didn't flinch! I was so proud of him in that moment! And again, as per my ex's usual, it was several months before we heard from him again.

I was a strong-willed, hard-headed teen. I did things my way and suffered the consequences later. I was attracted to the "Bad Boys". I craved excitement. I believed in the phrase- "Everything happens for a reason". I fully believe that God was preparing me to appreciate the kind of love that I was meant to have. God wanted me to appreciate the husband that I now have that loves me unconditionally. The husband that allows me to be myself without fear of being shamed or made fun of. The husband that protects my children from the manipulative ways of their father.

It has only been in the last few years that my stomach no longer drops when my ex calls me. I no longer dread the fight that is sure to come because the kids don't want to spend the weekend with him. Maybe those feelings have subsided because the kids are old enough to decide for themselves how much participation he gets in their lives. They have both told him how they feel and no longer let him manipulate them. They are 15 and 19 now, and I am so proud of the people they are becoming! Maybe because they realize that his main goal was to hurt me by forcing them to spend time with him. Either way, the three of us are stronger than we would have been if we had stayed. We are happier than we would have been if we had stayed. We all know what it means to be loved and cared for. They even have a little sister that they adore, and who looks up to them daily.

If you are in a physically abusive relationship, GET OUT! I know that is easier said than done, but your LIFE could depend on it. If you are in an EMOTIONALLY abusive relationship, GET OUT! Again, easier said than done, but your LIFE could still depend on it. Emotional Abuse can be so much harder than the physical. When you start to question your own sanity, because you have been manipulated to believe you are stupid, or immature, or useless, you are being emotionally abused. Emotional abuse doesn't always come from a spouse. It can come from an employer, a "friend", even a family member. The bottom line is: You know who you are. You know that God loves you. You know that there are safe places where you can go. Find one immediately. Put your trust in the Lord, and he will guide you through your struggles. I am the last person that any of our church family thought would stay faithful, but I can't imagine surviving any of the things this world had thrown at me without HIM. With HIM, I am an OVERCOMER!

REFLECTIONS OF AN OVERCOMER:

1. **Choosing the wrong person does not make us weak.** Oftentimes, we as women worry too much about what others think of us. We worry that ending a relationship appears as though we did not do our part or try hard enough. When abuse is involved, no amount of trying will fix it. We have to know when to "quit" and move on.

2. **Stay true to yourself and your beliefs.** You know who you are deep down, and you should never let anyone change that. You are also fearfully and wonderfully made, so take pride in that and learn to love yourself. Spend time in prayer and ask God to lead you and protect you.

3. **When you see the "Red Flags", listen to your gut.** Acknowledge them for yourself. Take action, seek advice from a friend or family member, seek counsel from a church leader or other professional, seek shelter.

4. **Seek resources and help.** There are many resources available to victims of domestic violence. Use them. (Resources also listed at the back of this book.)

5. **Do not be afraid to love again.** You are beautiful, inside and out, and allowing yourself to love and be loved is one of the most freeing, and empowering things you can do for yourself.

Author Portia Mills Henderson

Portia Mills Henderson

Portia Mills Henderson, of Lexington, North Carolina, is a mom, wife, and a veteran of the United States Navy. Portia overcame great odds to transform her life and birth an extraordinary business. In 2012, while working to heal from abuse and her past, Portia started a journey of self-care, both spiritually and naturally. Portia's natural and physical healing was intertwined by God. God took Portia on an amazing journey of learning that he has provided everything, in nature, for our skin care needs. With that knowledge, Portia developed a business called, Love Nina Beauty Products. Love Nina makes handcrafted natural and organic beauty products.

Portia knew this blessing was tied to her past. God lead Portia to use the proceeds from her business to help children in need. Love Nina Beauty Products is a proud sponsor of the World of Children Organization. World of Children Organization has been recognized, by the media, as the "Nobel Prize of Child Advocates" and is the only global organization and funding program that exclusively focuses on a broad range of children's issues; including health, education, safety, sexual abuse, and human rights. Through World of Children Organization, 100% of all public gifts go directly to support programs serving vulnerable children worldwide. Love Nina became a precious avenue for Portia to be an advocate for children.

Portia never wanted to bring children into this world and risk them living an abusive childhood, like she suffered; but God saw fit to bless her with children. Portia's business was named after her daughter, Nina. Through her healing process, God revealed, to Portia, that the name of her business meant, "Love the Little Girl." Portia encourages all survivors to be patient in the process and know that every day, God is working everything together for your good. He knows the plans He has for you, plans to give you hope and a future and plans to not harm you.

Portia knew that God ordered her steps and what was meant to destroy her would deliver others. Through a chain of events she met Chemeka Turner-Williams. Chemeka asked Portia if she wanted to tell her story. Portia thanks Chemeka for being obedient to the vision God gave her! All the glory and honor belongs to God!

To learn more about World of Children Organization, visit:
Worldofchildren.org
To shop and support Love Nina Beauty Products:
Loveninabeautyproducts.com
To connect with Author Portia Mills Henderson:
lovenina2006@gmail.com

OVERCOMING THE ENEMY WITHIN ME

I desired a deeper relationship with God and to understand who I was and what my purpose was on this earth. My biggest challenge was letting go of my past and in order to do that, I had to stop running from it and realize that God would not have allowed certain things, to occur in my life, if he was not going to use them for his Glory. I was a product of sexual abuse. I grew up in a domestic violence home.

I had a battle going on in my mind! I was shouting: "*Save me, O God; for the waters are come up to my neck. I sink in the miry depths, where there is no foothold. I have come into the deep waters; the floods engulf me. I am worn out calling for help; my throat is parched. My eyes fail, looking for my God.*" Psalm 69:1-3 NIV. I wanted to be transformed by God. My past was a weight that I no longer wanted to carry.

When you think of the title: *Surviving in Silence: Overcoming Domestic Violence*, what do you picture in your mind? My story has a different twist than most domestic violence survivors. I did not receive the blows, I gave them. I was a child trapped in a nightmare of domestic violence. I watched the blows being given; I watched my mom being beaten. Joyce

Meyer said, "telling your story takes away the devil's power over you." He no longer has power over me. I was a product of my environment. Darkness took me by the hand and lead me down a path that forever changed my life. Through the darkness, God was the beam of light guiding me. I thought I was walking alone, the first ten years of my life, but God was carrying me.

In order for you to truly know my story, I must start from the beginning. My story begins in 1976 with me naked in a cold bathtub at three years old. My brother and I would go next door and play. I can't remember who abused me. All I remember is that it was children. I cannot remember how long the abuse lasted, and I can't remember when I started repeating the act that was done to me. As I lived through this nightmare, I was also living in a domestic violence household. I was acting out and trying to deal with situations I had no way of knowing how to handle. I remember getting in trouble at school. I remember fighting and sitting in the hallway, being embarrassed as other students walked by. I remember drawing a picture, in the second grade, of a boy and girl kissing. As I think back on it, I wonder why no one helped me. No one reached out to me and asked me what was going on with me. I am thankful for current organizations, training and awareness seminars that help others identify when a child is in crisis and gets them the help they need. When I think back over my childhood, I know that it's only by the grace of God that I survived it all. I am still healing. I know that I will continue to heal, as I help others. Nobody wants to tell the ugly things that they have done in their life because it is shameful! People always think that adults sexually abuse children and they do, but the children turn around and abuse other children. This is what happened to me and the cycle goes on and on until it STOPS! Be mindful of your children! Ask questions! Stop the Cycle!

In 1983, I faced one of the most traumatic experiences of my life; I was nine years old. I had just witnessed my mom and dad fighting. My brother and I would run to the neighbors and call the police to come help my mom. My mom had a gun in the house and my grandmother took it because she told her someone was going to get hurt. I found the gun, at my grandmothers, one day when I was cleaning out her dresser drawers. My family lived in the projects. I told my mom that I saw her gun; never in my wildest dreams did I think the unthinkable would happen. On this particular night, my mom left out the house and turned towards my grandmother's house. My heart dropped! I knew my mom was going to get her gun. My 12-year-old brother and I ran towards my grandma's house as my mom was leaving out the house. I heard my grandma screaming, "Who told her where the gun was." It was me! Before my brother and I made it back home, we heard a gun firing off. I fell to my knees and knew my dad was dead. Fortunately, when she shot at him, she *missed.* However, that was the turn of events that made my mom decide to leave my dad. My mom was 26 at that time. Eventually, my mom and dad had a decent relationship and he asked for her forgiveness for all the things he had done to her.

My life stabilized after my mom and dad separated, but it came back full circle when I got in high school. I had suppressed a lot of the memories of my childhood. The sexual abuse, and the witnessed domestic violence all came crashing in on me during my high school years and I became suicidal. I was living in a secret Hell! I remember driving, one day, and saying to myself, "If I drive off this bridge the pain will go away!" One day, I was watching Oprah on tv and her daily topic was sexual abuse. I was in the 11th grade at this time. I cried as I heard the stories. My mom asked me had I ever been abused. I broke down and told her that I had been, but what was worst was that I had repeated it. I was broken. I told my mom I could not handle the memories of what happened when I was a child. My mom got me a counselor and that helped me greatly.

Deep inside of me, a domestic violence monster was buried! I found this out when I was in high school. When my boyfriend, who is now my husband, would make me angry, I would hit him. He was not brought up in a home where there was domestic violence. He did not have it in him to hit me back. On one occasion, I remember hitting him and he accidentally busted my lip trying to protect himself. He cried; it broke his heart that he had hurt me. It also broke mine and made me look at the person I had become. My dad was a product of domestic violence. He promised himself that he would never be that person. He ended up being the exact thing he hated. The cycle of abuse is real. I shudder when I think about the person I would be if God had not intervened in my life. God saved me from myself!

On December 20, 2004, we celebrated my son's seventh birthday. All day I felt down and depressed. Have you ever had that feeling that something was wrong, but you did not know what it was? I remember the police car pulling up to my house. As the police officer came up the walkway, he asked was I my dad's daughter? I knew he was going to tell me something had happened to my dad. My dad had been murdered by his girlfriend. She had stabbed him in his heart. Not only that, but she was on the run. They finally caught her four years later. They gave my dad's girlfriend only three years in prison because they deemed her insane. They called it a crime of passion. I have yet to talk to her or see her. I wanted to go see her in prison, but God would not allow me to go.

I was devastated by the loss of my dad. My dad had two sides to him. On one hand, he had a heart of gold and if I knew anything in this world, I knew he loved me. On the other hand, my dad was a man that could not drink alcohol. It turned him into another person and made him mean and abusive. I spoke with him the week before he was murdered, and he said that he needed to leave his girlfriend. After my dad died, there were reports that he and his girlfriend had broken up and she made comments that-, "If I can't have him, no one will." This is an example of your past following you. My dad had a history of domestic violence. No one knows what lead her to kill him. I remember, that one night, my dad and I were on the phone and I lead him in the prayer of salvation. I feel that in his last moments of life, he called on Jesus!

When he died, I couldn't help but to recall Matthew 26:52, "*For all who draw the sword will die by the sword.*" When I found out that they gave her only three years and the case would not go to trial, my heart was broken. I sobbed on the phone, as I told my mom the news. My mom said something to me that I will never forget. She said, "Listen to me! I tried to hurt your dad myself." She said, "I have scars on my face that only I can see." She told me to put his girlfriend in God's hands, forgive her and let God do a work in her. My mom is fair-skinned, and I remember her black eyes and her tears. One thing I often hear people say is that they stay in an abusive relationship for the kids. In my opinion, that is the worst thing a parent can do! I am a living witness. If it was not for the grace of God, I could've easily become an abuser, like my father. I can't help but think what type of man my dad would've been, if he didn't grow up in a home full of violence. I can't help but think what type of person I would be, if I didn't grow up in an abusive environment. I want people to realize that staying in an abusive relationship could lead to death and it could negatively affect your children for their entire lives; or worst, turn them into Abusers.

As an adult, I had to ask for forgiveness for what I did as a child. That was part of my healing. I had to lay down that heavy burden. One day, my mom and I were behind a bus, unloading kids at an elementary school. My mama said, "Look at those kids. Do you think they should be held accountable for things that happened to them that they could not control or things that they did?" She said, "Look at them. That was you!" I watched those kids get off the bus, with their little backpacks on, and I cried for me. I cried for the children that hurt me because they did not know what they were doing. One thing that I know is, in life, we can't change the past! I use to pray and ask God why I had to go through that as a child. I often wondered why I didn't tell someone what was happening to me. Maybe I did not know the words. If only……Now, I know it was all to help someone else.

My childhood affected every aspect of my life. The devil loved to whisper in my ear. The devil had a strong hold over me, and only God could set me free. I never felt good enough, never felt worthy of love, never felt deserving of anything good. When I had good moments, the devil would always plant conflicted thoughts in my mind; telling me I didn't deserve to be happy. Anything bad that happened to me, I would chalk it up as punishment for my past sins. I loved the Lord. On one hand, I would accept that I was forgiven; on the other, I felt like I was unforgivable! I recently heard a sermon, at church, that was titled- *Loving Your Enemy Even When The Enemy Is Yourself?*'

I went and spoke to my Bishop, when I was 40 years old. He showed me that I was forever punishing the little girl in me. He explained that I had never acknowledged or grieved what she went through. I had only acknowledged and grieved what she did as a result of her abuse. I had her sitting in the corner as I called her a "Bad Girl!" The Bishop said, "Forgive her!" I had a spiritual experience! It was as if the little girl crawled up in my lap and I hugged her and comforted her. I loved her and we cried together. She is lovable. God took my heart of stone and gave me a heart of flesh so I could truly feel. I had put my past to rest and it no longer had a hold over me. I knew God loved me and he wanted me to be happy and whole. I finally loved Portia. That day, I walked out of Bishop's office renewed in my spirit.

My husband and I have been together for 30 years and married for 22 years. I feel safe with him. My husband ultimately gave me a safe place to grow and heal. The little girl inside of me had to heal before I could be the person God called me to be, and truly walk in my purpose. What she endured was my purpose. I had to let God do his work in me so he could turn what was meant to destroy me into a catalyst that would break the chains off of others so they could be free! Because of the things I experienced as a child I sheltered my kids. They wanted to spend the night and go places with their friends. I would not let them go. I would get physically ill thinking about something happening to them. I explained to them that my job was to protect them. I have always been open with my kids about my childhood. I wanted them to understand why I was the way I was.

I know I went through all of the abuse when I was a child, to set someone free! It was never about me. I pray that someone finds healing from my story. Job 42:10 "*And the LORD turned the captivity of Job, when he PRAYED FOR HIS FRIENDS: also, the LORD gave Job twice as much as he had before. 12: So, the LORD blessed the latter end of Job more than his beginning!*" Our latter days will be greater than our former days! We must pray for one another, in doing so, we will find healing. I know my testimony will give someone else the strength to make it through another day. To let them know that you are not your past, your past is only part of your journey!

Writing this story has brought me more healing than I could've ever imagined. My past is my burnt offering to the Lord! 2nd Samuel 24:2: "*neither will I offer burnt offering unto the Lord my God of which doth cost me nothing!*" I paid this price for someone else's freedom. I am honored that God chose me to tell my story to help someone else be free! No matter what I went through in my life, my suffering is nothing compared to the price Jesus paid for all of us to be free! No matter what we face, in life, it is not bigger than our God! Psalms 62:5-8 "*My soul, wait thou only upon God; for my expectation is from him. He only is my rock and my salvation: he is my defense; I shall not be moved. In God is my salvation and my glory: the rock of my strength, and my refuge, is in God. Trust in him at all times; ye people, pour out your heart before him. God is a refuge for us, Selah!*"

I always reflect on the words of Myles Munroe "Life is short, and we better figure out our purpose!" When I die, I want to die *Empty*. I want to pour out everything God put in me to give to this world. I want to be a demonstration of God's work. Hold God's hand and let him heal you and transform you. You were born for a reason. God gives us the Grace and Mercy to walk in our purpose! I pray as you read my story it will lead you to the one true healer, "Jesus Christ." and you will be restored. Through Jesus Christ, I am an Overcomer!

REFLECTIONS OF AN OVERCOMER:

Insights that gave me Beauty for Ashes:

1. **I had to stop running from my past!** There was nothing I could do to change what happened to me or through me. I surrendered to God because he was the only one that could heal me.
2. **2nd Corinthians 12:9-11** "My Grace is sufficient for you, for my power is made perfect in weakness." God was my strength when I had none. When I was sad and could feel myself slipping into depression I would listen to worship music. I would also listen to pastors preach the word. Reading the word of God and going to church gave me the foundation I needed to start my path to healing. I kept my mind stayed on God.
3. **I was intentional in my Journey to healing.** I reached out to my Bishop, I went to encounters and talked to my friends and family for support. Don't be afraid to tell your story, you will find freedom and healing in telling it! It is yours to tell, not to be ashamed of or to keep it a secret! Keeping secrets will destroy you and give the devil a strong hold over you!
4. **Trust God!** It is one thing to say you trust him. It is a totally different thing to surrender and let him direct your path. When God is leading you and directing you to do certain things you must obey. For example, asking others for forgiveness!
5. **Forgiving myself!** This was one of the most difficult things I had to do. I could forgive others for hurting me, but could not forgive myself for hurting others. There is no way to move on until you learn to do this! Once I forgave myself, I started my true journey to wholeness. It will happen in a twinkling of an eye and you will realize God has given you Beauty for your ashes.

Author Evelyn Collins

Evelyn Collins

Evelyn Collins is a WARRIOR! A survivor of both domestic abuse and cancer. She wrote her story as a release and to be a blessing to someone else. Evelyn holds many titles; a Thespian, Soloist, Foster Parent, the first black female Law Enforcement Officer with NC Dept. of Insurance (retired), retired auditor and past mentor for domestic violence victims. Evelyn is currently nominated for *Best Actress* for the 8th Annual Playwrights Award. She is also a life-time member of the NAACP and Delta Sigma Theta Sorority.

Born the 15th of 18 children, Evelyn studied at Morgan State University in Baltimore, MD. She graduated from National University in La Jolla, California, with a bachelor's degree in accounting. She also holds a master's degree in Counseling from Capella University in Minnesota and has completed advanced graduate work at Capella University.

Of all her many accomplishments, Evelyn thanks God for her family! She is most thankful for her amazing daughter, son-in-law and two grandsons, who give their love and support all the time. Evelyn thanks Bud'da, her son-in-law, for allowing his wife, her daughter-Cassandra Anderson, to spend many nights encouraging her to write her story. Evelyn is most appreciative of Joshua W. Steward, for the many missed date nights, as she wrote and researched to draft her story. Evelyn salutes her 94-year-old mother, and her brothers and sisters. They are her motivators.

Evelyn prays that her story will be an encouragement to someone else to start their journey to overcome.

Email: Collins.evelyn@yahoo.com
Twitter: evelyncollins@evelyn15collins
Facebook: Evelyn Collins
Website: survivinginsilence.com

OVERCOMING THROUGH THE FIGHT TO REGAIN

As a child, something happened to me, and that abuse kept me running. Seduced by empty sweet talk, I usually ended up running straight into the arms of another abuser. I was abused physically by being whipped excessively, because I had a bedwetting problem. My parents said, like most parents of that era and some even today, especially if they don't have the means or like to go to the doctors, that my chronic bedwetting was due to my being lazy and not getting up. Their response was an almost daily whipping with a switch, until I was 13 years old, when the doctor told my parents that my bladder was too small for my age.

At the age of four-five years old, a family member started to touch me inappropriately. When my sister told my father that the family member was coming into our room at night, our father's response was; it was our fault because we needed to get fully dressed to go to the bathroom in the middle of the night; instead of in our slip and panties. From then on, I learned to be silent about my abuses, because I didn't want to draw any unwanted attention to myself. Then came the emotional abuse. I was teased and called names by my 17 siblings (yes, you read it right, there are 18 of us), because of my excessive bedwetting.

My siblings didn't know that I couldn't control the bedwetting, so they followed in my parents' design to further my abuse. I was called Pee Pot, Pissy; you name it. Then, there was the lone sheet on the clothesline. Everyone seemed to know what that meant. Or at least I thought so. I'm sure it was awful for my sisters because we slept two to a bed. And I was sure to wake every morning to the covers being snatched off and the whipping; it didn't make for pleasantries in the morning. The shame that I felt was so overwhelming that I barely remember much of my childhood.

I acted out and caused self-abuse by overeating for comforts sake. In my child's mind, I thought if I was bigger, the touching would stop. Since I didn't know how to make the sexual abuse or bedwetting stop, maybe the food would give me some comfort. This only made it worst. I have one sister that was so verbally abusive that she provoked my anger and made me just want to disappear. She'd walk up behind me and say something like- "You Big Black Pee Pot". I was enraged and would try to fight her. It was assumed that it was always my fault. So, eventually I learned to grow numb to the name calling and physical, mental and emotional abuse. This was the beginning of a long road of suffering in silence. There was no one I could talk to that would dare question my parents' authority.

Physical, mental, emotional abuse, along with guilt and shame dominated my life as a child. It became so overwhelming that I ran away from home at the age of 16, after a severe beating that I suffered one morning before school. This was in the days when girls wore dresses. My father had beat me that morning with his belt buckle because he saw me push my mother off me. She was slapping me in my face because she said I had sassed her. So, I pushed her back off me and tried to say I hadn't sassed her; but it was of no avail. I swore I would never stay in that house with those crazy people, so I ran away to my girlfriend's house. When I got there, her father said I couldn't stay with them because he didn't want to have to kill my father. So, my friend helped me move to another city to stay with one of her aunts. I didn't care where I went. If my father beat me that bad for what he perceived as abuse of my mother, imagine the hell that I would receive now that I had exposed some of the things going on in our house! In my young mind, anything was better than what was going on in my home. My bothers, and sisters; most of them older than I, would not come to my rescue because they didn't want to face the wrath of my father. I had no place to escape the pressure of the abuse.

I was so broken, I thought God had forsaken me because of the sexual abuse, even though it was not my fault. I didn't try anymore to seek His face and I could no longer hear His voice. My discerning spirit was dulled by the trauma of the abuse. I became an easy target. I was overjoyed when someone approached me and professed to love me. I had never really dated, so I never learned how to evaluate a man. I believed people were honest in their dealings. After all, mom and dad always let you know what they were going to do to you. So, if somebody says they love you, it must be true, right.... wrong!

Through all my abuses, I had to work. Work was a place of solace and gave me some of the few good memories I had of my childhood because my 17 siblings and I worked hard, but it had purpose. As kids, we saw how to build a strong legacy on the 200 acres farm my parents owned through their hard work. Today, my mom, along with some of us kids, still maintains ownership of some of that land.

My siblings and I would go to school on the first day, to register, and then be out of school for four to six weeks to harvest the crops. Education was second to survival in my father's eyes. After all, he had a third-grade education and owned 200 acres and rented another 50-60 acres to increase his profits. We worked the crops from the end of February until November. The only days we had off were when it rained and when we went to church. We were either planting the crop, harvesting the crop or coming out of the harvest season in the winter season. We raised most of our food, with the exception of sugar, flour, coffee, cheese, and molasses. We grew all fruits, vegetables, chicken, cows for beef and pigs for bacon, ham, sausage and lard for cooking. We canned or froze the fruits, vegetables and meats in season to have in the winter months.

I knew I needed an education to move beyond this kind of backbreaking labor. I was 17 when I got married the first time and gave birth to my daughter. I knew I had to get my degree to give her a better life. Her father was so abusive; he'd actually hit our daughter when he was trying to get to me during one of his fits of anger. I knew I needed to get away from him. One day he left to visit his parents. I'd already found another apartment. I moved and left no forwarding address. My parents' work ethic had created in me a determination and ability to work. I had missed the formative years of education while working in the fields, but my father had taught me how to do mental math and he gave me a strong business sense; which is what I always brought into my relationships. I suffered in silence about my struggle with academics, including writing, but determination and hard work kept me moving forward.

There came a point when I only needed 15 hours to complete my first degree. However, I had to postpone achievement of my goal and ended up spending the next three years standing by my man, when he moved to another state for a job promotion. I supported a husband who embarrassed me in front of family, friends, the children, co-workers, strangers and even the dog, with words like-*Whore, Slut, Bitch.* The profanity was profuse. He was like a man suffering from Tourette syndrome! To further add to my distress, when he got mad, he would even close down the bank accounts. My suffering in silence continued.

For years, I felt like I had betrayed the family by speaking up and exposing the family secrets. When I was much older, I told my mom about the sexual abuse. Her response was "If I'd known, I would have whipped both of you!" The irony of it; she knew. She had taught us to suffer in silence for the good of the family. On another occasion I called her after my husband, and I had a fight. She said- "teeth and tongue fall out sometimes." I no longer wanted to continue to be my husband's physical punching bag, curse out punching bag or financial punching bag. I no longer wanted to be controlled or manipulated; I had become a sponge of emotional abuse. I no longer desired to be vulnerable to the *fairytale savior* that my narcissistic husband presented himself as. In reality, my husband was the opposite of a savior. He had sized me up and ate away at my dreams, divided my family, crushed my good reputation, eliminated my hobbies, short -circuited my career and played with my sanity. On top of that, he had cheated on me, sometimes disappearing for days and then he would have the nerve to accuse me of doing the same! He would project his junk on me, and he had no shame in calling my relatives and telling lies to tarnish my character.

I can remember, initially in our relationship, thinking – "this man is special". I was shocked that he bought me all these gifts that I never asked for. I thought, "Wow, isn't that thoughtful!" He would call me 100 times a day, just to say sweet nothings. Now, his was the voice that insulted me or ignored me all together. He was a narcissist; but never in the presence of others. I had no earthly idea how the anger and alienation of affection started in the first place. When we'd get home from my family events, I quickly discovered that he just wanted to hoop-it-up with all my folks, and then return home to continue his silent treatment. Never ever did he allow me and *his* relatives to breathe the same air. I was always isolated. I had no idea he had begun a campaign against me with his family. I didn't like them. While he was sitting up in my momma, daddy, and siblings' faces, as if nothing was wrong, he was making plans against me.

Ironically, I did fight his punches, even though I was afraid. I was afraid of what I'd have to do to him to get him off me or what I'd conjure in my mind to do to him while he was asleep. Abuse is scary and debilitating. It's like walking on eggs shells or balancing on a tight rope. It's not only about the trauma of surviving; it's about how I might hurt someone in defense of my life. My abuser further victimized me by moving us away from my family. It was most painful being away from my daughter, grandkids and siblings. This isolation was used to keep me under control. It was not love.

It's nothing but God that allowed me to get an education. Growing in an abusive relationship is a whole other fight for a woman. I was trained to be submissive by my mother; in an indirect manner. As a result, I worked to be a great helpmate who cooked, cleaned, washed and ironed; I presented myself as devoted and smart. I helped my spouse get his position and supported and helped him build his business. I was the supportive wife for 20 years. Then when the business began to profit, I became expendable for the next *Flavor of the Day!* When you are hitched to the wrong man you will eventually be left by the wayside.

In my last relationship, I was instrumental in getting the homeowner, who was about to lose his home, to sign a quit claim deed to my husband and me. I was able to get the seller to agree to sell the house on paper, for more than he wanted. However, it was agreed, that after the closing, he would give us the difference, to enable us to make some much needed improvements. We did not have to put any money down and we got $35,000.00 at closing! While I was happily celebrating the deal, my husband was secretly conniving against me. My husband instructed the lawyers, after leaving the signing table, to take my name off the deed! I did not find out until ten years later! There were many other deals, in our 20-year marriage, where I helped package real estate transactions or increased contract lines of credit. When my husband would get all the information he needed, he would stop talking about the process and would even lie to say the deal fell through. I was not notified when the deals closed. I was left completely in the dark

To make sure I had no access to acquired property or funds, my husband used his daughter to forge my name, and his girlfriends' daughter to notarize the documents; alleging we were separated ten years before we actually separated. Through these devious methods, he obtained a loan on a property he did not want me to know about. This disallowed me access to the benefits I should have received as his spouse. While he worked hard to hide everything from me, he'd blow a gasket if I would buy an extra cracker, without their permission, even though, I was also working!

I was trained in law enforcement; perhaps God did this to give me silent ways to protect myself. I was trained as a tax auditor so I could always get a job or start my own business as needed. I was building my clientele when I met my husband; however, he insisted on being in my office, whenever I was in consultation with a client. Eventually, I lost all my clients because they did not feel comfortable being in the office with someone who was not involved in the preparation of their taxes. After all, it was a private consultation. I could never get my husband to see this, or he just didn't want to see it. If I had been successful perhaps, I would have moved forward a lot sooner.

It was the diagnosis of my breast cancer that allowed my voice to ring out and break the silence of my abuse inside my marriage. My therapist had a conference call with my family to discuss with them that my husband's narcissistic personality disorder (NPD) had caused him to treat me in abusive ways. The therapist confirmed that this had caused extreme stress on me; which may have caused the cancer. It was freeing! I no longer had to try to explain him or make excuses.

After my last relationship ended, and my bout with breast cancer, I realized, for my own health's sake, I could no longer suffer in silence. I knew that the silence of childhood abuse and hidden spousal abuse is killing many women today. I was fortunate; during all of my heartache and pain, God gave me the strength and determination to prosper. I completed high school, obtained a Bachelor of Accounting, and two master's degrees in counseling. I realized each trial made me stronger. They made me an overcomer. I lived it and I studied it. Mine is a classic story; for often, spousal/relationship abuse is connected to childhood abuse. Being honest, I was driven to understand life challenges, including my own; this encouraged me to get my counseling degrees to try to heal, and to be a blessing to others. Actually, when you are in pain, it's easier to help someone else, than face the pain in yourself. It allows you to take your mind off the pain of your own problem.

As I look back over my childhood and reflect on my family, I am blessed that things aren't what they used to be. My siblings and I are closer now, I've forgiven them, and know they would have helped to protect me, if they could. I write this because I have to own my story. My parents meant well; however, these things happened. I learned to mask my feelings. I'm not sure my siblings really knew all that I went through that caused me to run away from home and how the childhood abuse affected my entire life. So, I encourage everyone to find healing from damaging situations. Don't continue to bleed on unsuspecting strangers. By all means don't ignore abuse of any kind. I believe we continue to be a target for the enemy because he knows our story so well. After all, he is the one that sends abusers, misusers and manipulators to destroy our life, unless we have Jesus as our anchor. Face your demons before they destroy you.

As an overcomer, I celebrate the joy that is now in my life! God's voice not only allowed me to be free in performing in church, but also in theatrical gospel plays. I must admit that performing has brought me great mental healing and happiness. I know that God gave me this singing voice as my protection and a personal tool to praise God, in the darkest and toughest times of my storm.

Today, I am a survivor of mental, physical, social -economic, and narcissistic abuse. I no longer intend on suffering in silence. I'm on the road to staying healthy- mentally, and physically. I own my story and pray that it may free others. I am truly an OVERCOMER!

REFLECTIONS OF AN OVERCOMER:

So, what I can share that I've learned on my journey to *me* is -

1. **Control is not love.** However, it is a pathway to losing yourself, at the risk of becoming someone you may not recognize.
2. **Find true friends and a therapist that you can talk with in order to release the toxins from abuse.** Don't be afraid to say something. Don't worry about what others will say; instead focus on how they may pray for you or lead you to someone who can assist in your healing journey.
3. **God's discernment is required.** Narcissistic Abuse deals with a Lifetime Movie, top-of-the-line type of a manipulative spirit. The abuse will psychologically cause you to question your own sanity. This happens when there's an unusual amount of adoration and overboard Hallmark Show type of gift-giving; you must consider the authenticity of the giver's actions. You could find yourself, a year or two later, taking an abuser back, after one of his fits of rage. You must unpack your heart's condition and know that you need God more than man, to discern whether you've picked a true love or an abuser.
4. **Understand the signs of a narcissist.** Many narcissists like to do things to impress others, by making themselves look good externally. This "trophy" complex can exhibit itself physically, romantically, sexually, socially, religiously, financially, materially, professionally, academically, or culturally. In these situations, the narcissist uses people, objects, status, and/or accomplishments to represent the self, substituting for the perceived, inadequate "real" self. These grandstanding "merit badges" are often exaggerated. The underlying message of this type of display is: "I'm better than you!" or "Look at how special I am—I'm worthy of everyone's love, admiration, and acceptance!" Beware of the lows. No matter how good it feels on the highs, remember the lows are coming and they often get deeper and deeper. Even if someone has issues from childhood that predisposes them to abuse, it's not okay to continue. They need to get help. Please know, you may not be as fortunate the next time. Statistics show four women are killed by their intimate partner each day!

5. **You cannot save the abuser.** You can only save yourself. If you are being abused, seek help and get out of the situation. I pray that my story will help someone else make better decisions in relationships.

Author Di'Shawn Edwards

Di'Shawn Edwards

The child, Di'Shawn L. Edwards, whose name was chosen by father, Nelson Edwards and mother, Althea Edwards, was born on September 28, 1987 in Halifax County. She graduated from Weldon High School in 2005 and transitioned to Halifax Community College where she received a certificate of completion in Cosmetology. While pursuing her career of choice, she did so, mothering two young sons who observed and grew with her through the process. These two handsome young men are now 11 and 12 years of age. Di'Shawn grew up in Northampton County, North Carolina, in the small town of Seaboard. She traveled up and down the east coast from Virginia to Georgia before establishing residency in her home county of Northampton County where she is the gratified owner of the beauty salon that she established in 2015. Di'Shawn receives spiritual teachings from New Dimension Deliverance Ministries. She gives them credit for helping to guide her through her therapeutic healing process. Di'Shawn, also wishes to honor her four siblings who played major roles, at various stages in her life.

"Looking at life expectancy from diverse angles with different lenses, you will get an altered outlook of what you once saw" is the motto that takes Di'Shawn further into her healing process. She reflects on this thought daily and it serves to motivate her as she begins to reveal her truth. In deciding to finally speak on her truth, she had to endure and re-live scenarios that brought back pain, anger and bitterness. However, she believed that the purpose of the process of writing her story, was not only for her to re-evaluate herself and her growth, but to give hope to women who have been in similar circumstances or who are currently going through domestic abuse. Di'Shawn wishes for these women to know, that they too, can and will be able to unleash their truth!

OVERCOMING "THE LOVE"

"With time comes healing," they say, but I beg to differ!

With time comes pain, in time comes truth and as long as you have time you heal; is what I say. Being only 31, I get it! You're saying- "She's just a baby; she hasn't been though anything. She doesn't know what abuse could possibly be. Oh, she chose the wrong one and now she needs a plea". "But God," would be my response!

So, with me now knowing the different levels of abuse and knowing they each carry a different characteristic, sign and meaning, I had to pinpoint the source of my first level of emotional abuse. It took me back to my childhood. As a child I was often told different versions to explain why my mother was never around. As a child, I often wondered why I would call my aunt- *my mother*. As a child, I wondered why I wasn't good enough for my mother to care for me. These questions brought on emotional pain; they brought on silent cries and they kept my heart in a sheltered covering. As I got older, my mother would try to reach out by writing me letters and calling on the phone; but I had become numb. I had convinced myself that I really didn't need a mother who only wanted to deal with me when it was convenient for her. I remember stories being told by relatives; but the one I remember the most was about me being in high school and having a break down; an outpouring of my need for my mother's love. My mother was called, and when she answered the phone, I bombarded her with numerous questions as to why she had left me, and the response received was -."ask your father". Then there was a dial tone on the other end. I dried my tears, and right then and there, a barrier built up in me that was built with bricks of anger, hurt, betrayal, and lack of love. At that moment, I knew I had to find someone to love me and I had to find that person quickly! I was lacking the emotional love that I had never felt from my absent mother. My father was in my life, but he did not fill the void that I felt. Yes! I knew he loved me, and provided for me to the fullest, but actually saying- "I love you"; I never received. There were those times when the absorption of alcohol settled in his system and he would speak forcefully and with authority, trying to get me to understand that he was my main provider and I would never need anyone but him. So, it's safe to say that I had a trained mind when it came to love. The mindset of love was like the chain of demand; give me something and I will love you; don't give me anything and I will act like you never existed. This feeling of emptiness and loneliness caused me to go through fast friendships and relationships and then it attracted me to the first person who bought my love. Yes! Bought my love. I wasn't used to being shown this kind of "love". Being 17, working two jobs my last year of high school, this "love" made it known that - you can love me because I can afford you. The "love" bought me, and it triggered the mindset that I had been trained to view as love; love provides.

I believed; and this kind of love birthed two sons; my first son was conceived at 17 and my second son was conceived when I was 18. At this point, I believed I was living out my dream life. I have two healthy sons, I was working and attending college to attain my career goals. We had a house and vehicles and my sons' father had gotten out of the street life and stepped up and was working. The job was on the road and that meant no coming home Monday-Thursday; but that was okay. Life was perfect! I had finally found the emotional love that I had been seeking, and I would do anything to keep this "love." Outside looking in, people would agree that we were perfect; but on the inside a whirlwind was slowly forming. My sons' father was older than I was; I was underage; so that meant I was unable to attend the bars, nightlife spots and other places that he would decide to go without me. Now, I wasn't the type to question his whereabouts because when I went out, I wanted to go peacefully, as well. However, his nights started getting longer; then turned into coming home in the morning hours and eventually, not coming in at all. The alcohol use was getting heavier, but I didn't mention it because I didn't think it was my place. But this is where the verbal abuse crept in unaware. When mentioning accusations, whether wrong or right, it caused the drinking to become heavier. Yes, I did drink, but when there was a situation that required attentiveness, there was little to no alcohol consumed by me. I knew that I needed to be properly functioning and clear thinking to get effective results. As the situations escalated, I sometimes found myself displaying actions that were generated from pure rage and anger. His verbal nic-picking would sometimes cause me to throw the first blow. I would strike because I wasn't used to being talked down to like he talked to me. He never wanted to talk things out soberly. However, once he was heavily intoxicated, he suddenly wanted to *communicate*. These encounters almost always turned physical, where he would overpower me until a sound came forth of me gasping for air. Communicating was never of importance, so that meant the conversation ended that night and we would fall asleep, with the issue to never be spoken of again.

I remember that after most of the major attacks, there would be gifts. There would be new cars, a new home, designer jewelry, vacations; you name it. I was being bought to keep the outsiders happy and to keep the "love" alive. I was being bought to have this "love." I remember saying, I could the take the physical abuse better than the verbal abuse. With the physical abuse, I would fight back and try to protect myself, but the constant verbal abuse cut to the core. Both had me backing up from my career and going into a state of not wanting to work or be around people. So, I stayed isolated in the house, with the names he called me floating around in my head; holding me captive During this time I chose to let him be the head of the home; the sole provider; and I became the stay- at- home mom. But it really was depression settling in for a long stay. Suicide attempts started happening. I felt that I just needed this "love" so bad and if this "love" didn't want me, I would rather just die. I loaded a .45, and pulled the trigger, but the gun jammed. I called my older sister minutes before I pulled the trigger, because our bond was the closest and I just told her that I loved her so much and please take care of my sons. Then I hung up. I never told her where I was or what was going on, but soon after the gun jammed, my aunt busted through the door; thus, stopping me from trying again. My second attempt was by means of an overdose of medication. Almost lifeless, I laid in the hospital while they pumped my stomach. I wanted to end the pain of not being wanted; I wanted to end the pain of staying just because I didn't want to be another societal statistic. Then I figured I would take the easy way out. I become heavily intoxicated and got into my car and just accelerated to a dangerously high speed until I crashed the car. I crashed at a speed of almost 100 miles per hour! Being intoxicated, I woke up some time later, to discover that I was still very much alive, and the car only had muddy tires and a damaged front- end bumper. Why was either leaving this "love" or leaving this earth so hard to accomplish? I heard and saw newscasts about these things daily, but why couldn't I do it? So many things were running through my mind – "Why didn't my "love", love me the way I loved him? I didn't feel worthy of living if the "love" who I had so deeply fallen in love with didn't even recognize me; didn't want to be around me. There was almost no sex, and when he initiated it, it was so distasteful that my body didn't even yearn for his loving anymore. We had basically become roommates. I slowly got to a point where I started back working and focusing on my career. However, I stayed in faith that "this too shall pass" and my relationship with my "love" would improve. Time passed and nine years later I married him. Yes! I finally got what I wanted. I married him because after all we had been through, there was nothing left for the both of us to do. That is what I figured. We both had done our wrongs in the relationship and we weren't getting any younger. We both had flaws, some that were known to each other and some that were dismissed because all we knew was each other. We had basically grown up together and learned the ropes of life together. Some learnings had progressed us in our individual pursuits and others had hindered our minds from growing together.

But it some became clear that I had married a man who still wasn't ready; I married a man who never really asked to marry me. I just wanted love so badly that I was willing to pay for an entire wedding just because I wanted the love, he showed others. He was so unselfish, so caring about their problems, so willing to lend a helping hand; he was the perfect man to others, and I just needed him to be the perfect man for me. I wanted his "love" so badly, that this time it opened the door for me to embrace drug use, and I used drugs frequently. Unfortunately, they gave me the spirit of manipulation, witchcraft, and uncertainty. The drug use exposed me to a different lifestyle and the physical, emotional and verbal abuse could no longer be hidden from my family, friends, co-workers, or strangers. I had made up in my mind that I was all in for my marriage and if this was what I had to do to spend time with my husband, then so be it. My appearance was altered, my talk transformed, and my greed for worldly possessions became a need. My business was on the verge of failing, and my boys had seen so much at this point; behavior from both parents that they should have never witnessed. I didn't care; I was all in for my "love". That was until my body started rejecting the alcohol, prescription medications, ecstasy, a form of MDMA and the other *enhanced* street drugs. My health became a serious matter. My declining health took a toll on my marriage. The mental and physical health issues that I was going through were not understood by my "love." On our third-year anniversary, we vacationed like always, but this time I knew that my "love" didn't have any love for me anymore. While peeping through the door, in our hotel room, I watched him spike my drink with MDMA, which is a form of a street drug called, Molly. Knowing my health issues and the medications I was on, I knew that if this street drug entered my body, there really wouldn't have been much hope for me. So, I faked an asthma attack after pretending to drink that spiked drink. Instead of my husband rushing me to the hospital to seek immediate medical attention, he drove for hours and passed numerous medical facilities just to take me home to get an inhaler! This showed me that he had no desire to love me; but rather to let me die and cover up his wrongdoing by giving me the drug that had already done harm to my body. I was heartbroken out of this world! To me, this was the ultimate betrayal! Even after confronting him, and disclosing what I had done in the episode, the only thing he could look at me and say was that the sex was better when I performed sexual acts that I couldn't possibly tolerate unless under the influence of the drug. This type of abuse was above all else that I had previously encountered, and I knew at that moment that it was a *done deal.* I thought of my boys who looked to me for their well-being. They had seen blood pouring from my scraped knees and raised scars all across my body. My blood was left in trails, from me being pulled from my car and then being dragged into the home to be told to perform sexual acts and fulfill my husband's desires, against my will. My boys had heard their father calling me- "Bitch and Whore", while he phoned others to tell them how my behavior was childish, and I was not fulfilling the duties of a wife. It was in that moment that I couldn't stomach to see my boys hurt any more: it was a pain that cut so deep in my heart.

I had always been told; God would make a way of escape, but you have to be willing to take it. My desire for God was at an all-time low, in this deep hole that I was in. I had left my childhood church and I was seeking all kinds of support outside of my norm; I had strayed from God, but not forgotten Him. I remember the last time I was on a high, I just cried to the Lord saying, "I need help! You are the only one who can fix this relationship. "I need to be loved whole-heartedly from the inside out; with or without him." I drove to the doors of New Dimension Deliverance Ministries; high, out of my mind! Yet, a little piece of soberness, somewhere in my body, kept crying out for help. As I opened the doors and sat down on the front row; eyes bulging, rocking back and forth, skin feeling like it was on fire and licking my lips due to the reaction of the drugs, I remember the pastor looking over at me and gathering the elders around me saying- "NO, he can't have you like this!"

As a young girl, I always was in the church, so I always knew God; I always knew he was around me and I always knew that he was preparing me for something greater; even in my darkest times. This time, when I presented myself before the Lord, it was different. The sound was unfamiliar, and the change was drastic; the call for help was powerful because the relationship was on another level. This time I had to watch God strip me from head to toe even while in the presence of my newfound enemies. I had to start a new season with forgiving not only myself mentally, but completely and to forgive the people who played a role in my mistaken "love". I was on a quest for love not knowing that the whole time I had love. I just didn't know how to use it; I didn't know how to care for it, I didn't even know the purpose of this "love". So, as of today, I am divorced and yet, still healing from my "love". God is shaping and molding me to be the woman of love who he needs me to be. It goes back through 31 years of emotional, physical, and mental abuse. Not only was I a willing participant in some scenarios, but others played a major role as well. I can't speak personally for them, but what I do know is that with time comes pain, in time comes truth and as long as you have time you can heal daily. Use your time to become an OVERCOMER!

REFLECTIONS OF AN OVERCOMER:

In going forth and leaving my past and continuing to look for an optimistic future, I will leave you with this:

1.) Always make sure you love yourself. Loving yourself means never let anyone say that thinking of you is selfish. It's not! You have to learn to deal with your own battles, and cope through the pressures of not taking the easy road out or maneuvering through life and just setting the issues to the side.

2.) **Learn to deal with matters.** Even if it means going back to where it started and making that your starting point. It is important to address the issues. Don't move until you feel that the issue is resolved.

3.) **Stay close to your God.** Stay in his realm and never be so bound that you can't give him a praise; whether you're going through a valley or maintaining above level.

4.) **You must share your truth!** The things that we go through are not for us, but for others. I've learned a lot, as I overcame my countless life challenges. I've dealt with self-hurt, have hurt others, been abused, done the abusing. I've closed doors and opened doors. I have lived through guilt, shame, betrayal, unhappiness, adultery, disloyalty, unfaithfulness and deceitfulness, but my story has POWER! I pray that my struggles bless others. As you read my truth, I pray that it helps you to rise up out of any fear that has set in and pushes you pass any distress in your life. You, too should open up and start sharing your truth; sharing your testimony. It is freeing to release the things that have weighted us down.

5.) **Finally, you must take full responsibility for your mistakes**. Learn from them, grow daily and self-reflect on your actions. Take time to honestly forgive yourself and others and heal. Know that you are a woman with purpose and there is none like you.

I overcame with understanding that everybody is not going to understand, everybody is not going to love me the same, and nobody is going to offer or sacrifice the same as I. I had to overcome to be changed, and my purpose for changing was to become an OVERCOMER!.

Over the past decade a grave awareness has come to light when the subject of Domestic Violence is discussed. From the silent screams of the desperate house wife, the red blush bruises of the distressed girlfriend, the broken nails and lost high heel of the fleeing high school teenage lover, and the dark rings that cover the eye {eyes} of the battered woman are uncommonly common, since the beginning of time. There are millions of pillow cases, sheets, Kleenexes, and handkerchiefs that carry the DNA of the tears of those who have "Survived in Silence". Only if the tears that are mixed with eyeliner, mascara, and blood could talk. No matter how we address domestic violence or bring awareness to this matter, it {domestic violence} isn't ever a soothing conversation. Even though the bruises are similar, the assaults appear congruent, the pains {mentally, emotionally, and physically} are never the same. In this book {Surviving in Silence} we see a variety of perspectives surrounding domestic violence and the survival of each victim.

The visionary, Chemeka Williams, skillfully gathered a platoon of brave, surviving women, who carefully etched out a piece of their lives and put it into each chapter. What better way to learn how to survive than to seek the guidance and hear the stories of those who have sustained against the hardships of various forms of domestic violence. Chemeka Williams reveals that blood, sweat, and tears are not just bodily fluids, but they are tools used to survive the worst seasons of your lives; that are begot by the hands of those who should love you. Get ready to be revived as you recognize you are a survivor.

Pastor Orin Perry- The House of Mandate Inc.

RESOURCES FOR VICTIMS, SURVIVORS, & FAMILIES

Scriptures on Healing From Abuse

Scriptures on Healing From Abuse

"Husbands, love your wives and be not bitter against them" (KJV Colossians 3:19)

There are never any reasons or excuses for any form of violence and abusive behavior. It should never be acceptable and woven in you daily routine. I encourage you to seek proper help and get the necessary protection from any person that it inflicting abuse. Remember if someone is abused mentally, verbally, sexually, or physically it is NEVER their fault, nor is it ever justified. You are not the blame no matter what has been spoken to you. Biblical submission does not include having to take abuse in any form.The world that we live in has become all about control and enslavement, BUT the Lord is all about deliverance, freedom, healing and peace. Ultimately, God is a deliverer. Believe in Him and listen for His guidance. He will DELIVER you and then He will HEAL you. You must know and believe that the Almighty God LOVES you. He knows the pain and sees the tears and He is fighting on your behalf. You are fearfully and wonderfully made in the image of Jesus Christ. When you truly begin to see yourself as God does, you will not allow anyone to devalue, mishandle you or treat you any less than what you are. You are worthy of better, you are worthy of respect and YOUR LIFE MATTERS. You are a child of the Most High God.

Here are some scriptures to read and recite daily for strength and peace:

1. Psalm 34:18 (KJV) "The Lord is nigh unto them that are of a broken heart; and saveth such as be of a contrite spirit."

2. Psalm 51:6 (KJV) "Behold, thou desirest truth in the inward parts: and in the hidden part thou shalt make me to know wisdom."

3. Psalm 139:14 (KJV) "I will praise thee; for I am fearfully and wonderfully made: marvellous are thy works; and that my soul knoweth right well. My substance was not hid from thee, when I was made in secret, and curiously wrought in the lowest parts of the earth."

4. 2 Corinthians 3:17(KJV) "Now the Lord is that Spirit: and where the Spirit of the Lord is, there is liberty."

5. 1 John 4:18 (KJV) "There is no fear in love; but perfect love casteth out fear: because fear hath torment. He that feareth is not made perfect in love."

6. Psalm 63:3(KJV) "Because thy loving kindness is better than life, my lips shall praise thee."

7. Romans 8:37-39 (KJV) "Nay, in all these things we are more than conquerors through him that loved us. For I am persuaded, that neither death, nor life, nor angels, nor principalities, nor powers, nor things present,

nor things to come, Nor height, nor depth, nor any other creature, shall be able to separate us from the love of God, which is in Christ Jesus our Lord."

8. Isaiah 61:1-3 (KJV) "The Spirit of the Lord God is upon me; because the Lord hath anointed me to preach good tidings unto the meek; he hath sent me to bind up the brokenhearted, to proclaim liberty to the captives, and the opening of the prison to them that are bound; To proclaim the acceptable year of the Lord, and the day of vengeance of our God; to comfort all that mourn; To appoint unto them that mourn in Zion, to give unto them beauty for ashes, the oil of joy for mourning, the garment of praise for the spirit of heaviness; that they might be called trees of righteousness, the planting of the Lord, that he might be glorified."

9. Jeremiah 31:3 (KJV)"The Lord hath appeared of old unto me, saying, Yea, I have loved thee with an everlasting love: therefore with lovingkindness have I drawn thee."

10. Romans 8:14-16(KJV) "For as many as are led by the Spirit of God, they are the sons of God. For ye have not received the spirit of bondage again to fear; but ye have received the Spirit of adoption, whereby we cry, Abba, Father. The Spirit itself beareth witness with our spirit, that we are the children of God:"

11. John 10:10 (KJV)“The thief cometh not, but for to steal, and to kill, and to destroy: I am come that they might have life, and that they might have it more abundantly.”

12. Psalms 9:9 (KJV)“The Lord also will be a refuge for the oppressed, a refuge in times of trouble.”

13. Psalms 10:17-18 (KJV)“Lord, thou hast heard the desire of the humble: thou wilt prepare their heart, thou wilt cause thine ear to hear: To judge the fatherless and the oppressed, that the man of the earth may no more oppress.”

14. Genesis 50:20 (KJV) “But as for you, ye thought evil against me; but God meant it unto good, to bring to pass, as it is this day, to save much people alive.”

15. Psalms 34:18 (KJV)“The Lord is nigh unto them that are of a broken heart; and saveth such as be of a contrite spirit.”

16. Psalms 82:3(KJV) “Defend the poor and fatherless: do justice to the afflicted and needy.”

17. Psalms 107:20(KJV) “He sent his word, and healed them, and delivered them from their destructions.”

18. 1 John 3:20 (KJV)“For if our heart condemn us, God is greater than our heart, and knoweth all things.”

19. Psalms 145:14(KJV) “The Lord upholdeth all that fall, and raiseth up all those that be bowed down.”

20. Psalms 147:3(KJV) “He healeth the broken in heart, and bindeth up their wounds.”

21. Proverbs 10:11(KJV) “The mouth of a righteous man is a well of life: but violence covereth the mouth of the wicked.”

22. Isaiah 40:29-31(KJV)“He giveth power to the faint; and to them that have no might he increaseth strength. Even the youths shall faint and be weary, and the young men shall utterly fall: But they that wait upon the

Lord shall renew their strength; they shall mount up with wings as eagles; they shall run, and not be weary; and they shall walk, and not faint."

23. Isaiah 53:5 (KJV) "But he was wounded for our transgressions, he was bruised for our iniquities: the chastisement of our peace was upon him; and with his stripes we are healed."

24. Isaiah 54:14-15 (KJV) "In righteousness shalt thou be established: thou shalt be far from oppression; for thou shalt not fear: and from terror; for it shall not come near thee. Behold, they shall surely gather together, but not by me: whosoever shall gather together against thee shall fall for thy sake."

25. Isaiah 61:3 (KJV) "To appoint unto them that mourn in Zion, to give unto them beauty for ashes, the oil of joy for mourning, the garment of praise for the spirit of heaviness; that they might be called trees of righteousness, the planting of the Lord, that he might be glorified."

26. Malachi 2:13-15 (KJV) "And this have ye done again, covering the altar of the Lord with tears, with weeping, and with crying out, insomuch that he regardeth not the offering any more, or receiveth it with good will at your hand. Yet ye say, Wherefore? Because the Lord hath been witness between thee and the wife of thy youth, against whom thou hast dealt treacherously: yet is she thy companion, and the wife of thy covenant. And did not he make one? Yet had he the residue of the spirit. And wherefore one? That he might seek a godly seed. Therefore take heed to your spirit, and let none deal treacherously against the wife of his youth."

27. Matthew 5:4(KJV)"Blessed are they that mourn: for they shall be comforted."

28. Matthew 11:28(KJV) Come to me, all who labor and are heavy laden, and I will give you rest.

29. Matthew 15:18((KJV)"But those things which proceed out of the mouth come forth from the heart; and they defile the man."

30. Matthew 18:10(KJV)"Take heed that ye despise not one of these little ones; for I say unto you, That in heaven their angels do always behold the face of my Father which is in heaven.

31. Psalms 82:4 (KJV) "Deliver the poor and needy: rid them out of the hand of the wicked."

32. Deuteronomy 32:10-12(KJV)"He found him in a desert land, and in the waste howling wilderness; he led him about, he instructed him, he kept him as the apple of his eye. As an eagle stirreth up her nest, fluttereth over her young, spreadeth abroad her wings, taketh them, beareth them on her wings:"

33. Luke 10:19(KJV)"Behold, I give unto you power to tread on serpents and scorpions, and over all the power of the enemy: and nothing shall by any means hurt you."

34. John 8:16 (KJV) "And yet if I judge, my judgment is true: for I am not alone, but I and the Father that sent me."

35. John 14:27(KJV) "Peace I leave with you, my peace I give unto you: not as the world giveth, give I unto you. Let not your heart be troubled, neither let it be afraid."

36. Romans 12:17-21 (KJV) "Recompense to no man evil for evil. Provide things honest in the sight of all men."If it be possible, as much as lieth in you, live peaceably with all men." Dearly beloved, avenge not yourselves, but rather give place unto wrath: for it is written, Vengeance is mine; I will repay, saith the Lord. Therefore if thine enemy hunger, feed him; if he thirst, give him drink: for in so doing thou shalt heap coals of fire on his head. Be not overcome of evil, but overcome evil with good."

37. 1 Corinthians 13:4-7 (KJV) "Charity suffereth long, and is kind; charity envieth not; charity vaunteth not itself, is not puffed up, Doth not behave itself unseemly, seeketh not her own, is not easily provoked, thinketh no evil; Rejoiceth not in iniquity, but rejoiceth in the truth; Beareth all things, believeth all things, hopeth all things, endureth all things."

38. II Corinthians 1:3, 4(KJV)"Blessed be God, even the Father of our Lord Jesus Christ, the Father of mercies, and the God of all comfort; Who comforteth us in all our tribulation, that we may be able to comfort them which are in any trouble, by the comfort wherewith we ourselves are comforted of God."

39. II Corinthians 2:14 (KJV) "Now thanks be unto God, which always causeth us to triumph in Christ, and maketh manifest the savour of his knowledge by us in every place."

40. Psalms 57:1(KJV) "Be merciful unto me, O God, be merciful unto me: for my soul trusteth in thee: yea, in the shadow of thy wings will I make my refuge, until these calamities be overpast."

41. Ephesians 4:29-32 (KJV)"Let no corrupt communication proceed out of your mouth, but that which is good to the use of edifying, that it may minister grace unto the hearers. And grieve not the holy Spirit of God, whereby ye are sealed unto the day of redemption. Let all bitterness, and wrath, and anger, and clamour, and evil speaking, be put away from you, with all malice: And be ye kind one to another, tenderhearted, forgiving one another, even as God for Christ's sake hath forgiven you."

42. Isaiah 43:4(KJV) "Since thou wast precious in my sight, thou hast been honourable, and I have loved thee: therefore will I give men for thee, and people for thy life."

43. II Timothy 1:7(KJV) "For God hath not given us the spirit of fear; but of power, and of love, and of a sound mind."

44. John 14:27 (KJV)"Peace I leave with you, my peace I give unto you: not as the world giveth, give I unto you. Let not your heart be troubled, neither let it be afraid."

45. Hebrews 4:16(KJV) "Let us therefore come boldly unto the throne of grace, that we may obtain mercy, and find grace to help in time of need."

46. Hebrews 13:6(KJV) "So that we may boldly say, The Lord is my helper, and I will not fear what man shall do unto me."

47. James 4:7 (KJV) "Submit yourselves therefore to God. Resist the devil, and he will flee from you."

48. Exodus 14:14(KJV) "The Lord shall fight for you, and ye shall hold your peace."

49. II Corinthians 12:9 (KJV) "And he said unto me, My grace is sufficient for thee: for my strength is made perfect in weakness. Most gladly therefore will I rather glory in my infirmities, that the power of Christ may rest upon me."

50. Micah 7:18-19 (KJV) "Who is a God like unto thee, that pardoneth iniquity, and passeth by the transgression of the remnant of his heritage? he retaineth not his anger forever, because he delighteth in mercy. He will turn again, he will have compassion upon us; he will subdue our iniquities; and thou wilt cast all their sins into the depths of the sea."

Education & Prevention of Domestic Violence

EDUCATION AND PREVENTION

"Types of Abuse and the Characteristics"

WHAT IS DOMESTIC VIOLENCE?

According to the United States Department of Justice Office on Violence Against Women, the definition of domestic violence is a pattern of abusive behavior in any relationship that is used by one partner to gain or maintain control over another intimate partner. The Center for Disease Control and Prevention defines it as the victimization of an individual with whom the abuser has an intimate or romantic relationship. The Centers for Disease Control and Prevention defines **domestic** as "physical violence, sexual violence, stalking, and psychological aggression (including coercive acts) by a current or former intimate partner." Domestic violence is a SECRET and UNNOTICED epidemic that is increasing globally at an alarming rate with traumatic and adverse health effects on individuals, families, and communities. This social disease has quietly integrated itself into the blueprint of our society.

Domestic violence is a problem that affects and impacts millions of people in all types of relationships. Domestic violence does not have any boundaries nor does it discriminate. It does not have any economic, occupational or educational status, gender, race, sexual orientation, nationality or religious limits. Domestic Violence/Abuse has often been stereotypically portrayed in only one perspective and that is physical violence. When most people visualize domestic violence they create an image where the abuser physically hurts the victim. Although, physical violence is one form of domestic violence, there are actually various types of domestic violence. It can be physical, emotional/mental, sexual, economic/financial, psychological(including threats of violence and physical harm, attacks against property or pets and other acts of intimidation, emotional abuse, isolation, and use of the children as a means of control), technological and stalking. Being subjected to any form of domestic violence can is damaging psychologically, leaving feelings of helplessness, low self-esteem, and even self-doubt. It's important that you understand what is domestic violence and the different signs of abuse so that you can quickly identify the problem and seek the necessary help.

FORMS OF ABUSE

Adopted by the National Coalition Against Domestic Violence

Physical Abuse: ***According to the National Coalition Against Domestic Violence*** Physical abuse includes the physical assault, battery, and sexual assault used as part of a systematic pattern of power and control perpetrated by one intimate partner against another. Physical abuse can cause severe injury and even death. It often co-occurs with other forms of abuse, including psychological abuse, economic abuse, and stalking.

Physical Abuse Includes: The use of physical power which results in injury, disability, or death are forms of physical violence. Other forms of physical violence include coercion, administering drugs or alcohol without permission, and denying medical care.

- ❏ Assault
- ❏ Restraining
- ❏ Scratching
- ❏ Shaking
- ❏ Shoving
- ❏ Slapping
- ❏ Pulling Hair
- ❏ Biting
- ❏ Burning
- ❏ Choking
- ❏ Gagging
- ❏ Grabbing
- ❏ Kicking
- ❏ Punching

Statistics of Physical Abuse: According To The National Coalition Against Domestic Violence

- More than 10 million Americans are victims of physical violence annually.
- 20 people are victims of physical violence every minute in the United States.
- 1 in 3 women and 1 in 4 men is a victim of some form of physical violence by an intimate partner during their lifetimes.
- 76% of intimate partner physical violence victims are female; 24% are male.
- 1 in 7 women and 1 in 18 men are severely injured by intimate partners in their lifetimes.
- Domestic violence accounts for 15% of all violent crime in the United States.

Why it Matters?

- Intimate partner physical abuse is not bound by age, socioeconomic status, race, ethnicity, sex, sexual orientation, gender identity, religion or nationality; it exists in all communities. Contrary to popular belief, physical abuse is not simply a maladjusted person's occasional expression of frustration or anger, nor is it typically an isolated incident. Physical abuse is a tool of control and oppression and is a choice made by one person in a relationship to control another.

Effects of Physical Abuse:

- Women abused by their intimate partners are more vulnerable to contracting HIV or other STI's due to forced intercourse or prolonged exposure to stress
- Studies suggest that there is a relationship between intimate partner violence and depression and suicidal behavior

- Physical, mental, and sexual and reproductive health effects have been linked with intimate partner violence including adolescent pregnancy, unintended pregnancy in general, miscarriage, stillbirth, intrauterine hemorrhage, nutritional deficiency, abdominal pain and other gastrointestinal problems, neurological disorders, chronic pain, disability, anxiety and post-traumatic stress disorder (PTSD), as well as noncommunicable diseases such as hypertension, cancer and cardiovascular diseases.
- Victims of domestic violence are also at higher risk for developing addictions to alcohol, tobacco, or drugs.

1. National Coalition Against Domestic Violence (NCADV). (2015). "Domestic Violence" Facts About Domestic Violence and Physical Abuse: Fact Sheet. Retrieved from www.ncadv.org. and pdf

Sexual Abuse: ***According to the National Coalition Against Domestic Violence***

Sexual violence is using physical coercion to force participation in unwanted sex acts, sexual touching, or a non-physical sexual event (e.g., sexting) when the partner does not or cannot consent. Perpetrators often incapacitate victims with alcohol or drugs. Perpetrators who are physically violent toward their intimate partners are often sexually abusive as well. Victims who are both physically and sexually abused are more likely to be injured or killed than victims who experience one form of abuse. Abusers assault people of all genders, races, ages, social classes and ethnicities. Women who are disabled, pregnant or attempting to leave their abusers are at greatest risk for intimate partner rape

Sexual Abuse Includes:

- Forced anal, oral, or vaginal penetration of a victim
- Forced penetration of someone else
- Sexual coercion involving intimidation to pressure consent
- Unwanted exposure to pornography, harassment, sexual violence, filming, taking, or disseminating sexual photograph or video
- Unwanted sexual contact

Statistics:

- 1 in 5 women will be raped in her lifetime. Nearly 1 in 2 women and 1 in 5 men experienced sexual violence victimization other than rape at some point in their lives.
- Intimate partner sexual assault and rape are used to intimidate, control and demean victims/survivors of domestic violence. Intimate partner sexual assault is more likely than stranger or acquaintance assault to cause physical injury.
- Between 14% and 25% of women are sexually assaulted by intimate partners during their relationship. Between 40% and 45% of women in abusive relationships will also be sexually assaulted during the course of the relationship.
- Women who are sexually abused by intimate partners report more risk factors for intimate partner homicides than non-sexually abused women
- 18% of female victims of spousal rape say their children witnessed the crime. Between 10% and 14% of married women will be raped at some point during their marriages. Only 36 percent of all rape victims ever report the crime to the police. Marital rape is the most underreported form of sexual assault.
- A majority of child victims are 12-17. Of victims under the age of 18: 34% of victims of sexual assault and rape are under age 12, and 66% of victims of sexual assault and rape are age 12-17.

How to Help

- Encourage primary care physicians and OB/GYNs in your community to screen women for signs of physical and sexual violence, and ask if they are in violent or abusive relationships during regular checkups.
- Demand state legislators update rape laws to include marital rape rather than considering marital rape a different crime.

- Work with local schools, religious youth groups, and other youth-oriented programs to teach about healthy sexuality and healthy relationships.

- ❑ Ask local schools and universities to address the issue of sexual violence in their classrooms and through victim assistance programs.
- ❑ Ask your members of Congress to support funding for direct surveys and programs created in the Violence Against Women Act.
- ❑

Effects of Sexual Abuse

- ❑ Post-traumatic stress disorder (PTSD), including flashbacks, nightmares, severe anxiety, and uncontrollable thoughts
- ❑ Depression, including prolonged sadness, loss of energy, feelings of hopelessness, unexplained crying, weight loss or gain or interest in activities previously enjoyed
- ❑ Suicidal thoughts or attempts. If you or someone you know is feeling suicidal, contact the National Suicide Prevention Lifeline at 1.800.273.8255.
- ❑ Dissociation, including not being able to focus at work or school.

Coalition Against Domestic Violence (NCADV) (2017). "Domestic Violence" Facts about Domestic violence and sexual assault: Fact Sheet. Retrieved from www.ncadv.org and pdf.

Economic/Financial Abuse: ***According to the National Coalition Against Domestic Violence***

When an abuser takes control of or limits access to shared or individual assets or limits the current or future earning potential of the victim as a strategy of power and control, that is economic abuse. In economic abuse the abuser separates the victim from their own resources, rights and choices, isolating the victim financially and creating a forced dependency for the victim and other family members.

Economic Abuse Includes:

Employment-related abuse: when the abuser prevents a victim from earning money. Examples include:

- ❑ Preventing victim from attending a job
- ❑ Demanding that the victim quits his or her job
- ❑ Preventing the victim from looking for jobs or attending job interviews
- ❑ Harassing the victim at work

Coerced debt: when an abuser forces non-consensual, credit-related transactions. Examples include:

- ❑ Applying for credit cards, obtaining loans, or opening accounts in a victim's name without their knowledge or consent
- ❑ Forcing the victim to obtain loans
- ❑ Forcing the victim to sign financial documents
- ❑ Use of threats or physical force to convince victims to make credit-related transactions
- ❑ Refinancing a home mortgage or car loan without a victim's knowledge

Other forms of economic abuse involve the abuser preventing a victim from accessing existing funds. Examples include:

- ❑ Deciding when or how the victim can access or use cash, bank accounts, or credit cards
- ❑ Forcing a victim to give the abuser money, ATM cards, or credit cards
- ❑ Demanding that the lease or mortgage or assets be in the abuser's name
- ❑ Using victim's checkbook, ATM card, or credit cards without the victim's knowledge
- ❑ Withholding finances to take care of basic needs

Economic Abuse Statistics:

- ❑ Between 94-99% of domestic violence survivors have also experienced economic abuse.
- ❑ Between 21-60% of victims of domestic violence lose their jobs due to reasons stemming from the abuse.
- ❑ Victims of domestic violence lose a total of 8 million days of paid work each year.
- ❑ Between 2005 and 2006, 130,000 stalking victims were asked to leave their jobs as a result of their victimization.

Why It Matters?

- ❑ Victims of domestic violence may be unable to leave an abusive partner or may be forced to return to an abusive partner for economic reasons.
- ❑ Victims of coerced debt may face massive barriers to economic self-sufficiency, including struggling to find a job or even obtaining a place to live after leaving an abuser due to debt and its detrimental effects on their personal credit score

National Coalition Against Domestic Violence (NCADV). (2015). "Domestic Violence" Facts about domestic violence and economic abuse. Fact Sheet. Retrieved from www.ncadv.org and pd

Psychological Abuse(Emotional or Mental Abuse): ***According to the National Coalition Against Domestic Violence***

Psychological abuse, often called emotional or mental abuse, is a form of abuse, characterized by a person subjecting or exposing another person to behavior that may result in psychological trauma, including anxiety, chronic depression, or post-traumatic stress disorder. I also involves trauma to the victim caused by the use of verbal and non-verbal communication with the intent to harm another person mentally or emotionally and/or exert control over another person. Psychological abusers use psychological abuse and tactics to manipulate, control, terrorize, and humiliate their victims over a period of time. It frequently occurs prior to or concurrently with physical or sexual abuse.

Psychological Abuse Includes:

- ❑ Humiliating the victim
- ❑ Controlling what the victim can or cannot do
- ❑ Withholding information from the victim
- ❑ Deliberately doing something to make the victim feel diminished or embarrassed
- ❑ Isolating the victim from friends and/or family
- ❑ Denying the victim access to money or other basic resources
- ❑ Stalkinging
- ❑ Demeaning the victim in public or in private
- ❑ Undermining the victim's confidence and/or sense of self-worth
- ❑ Convincing the victim (s)he is crazy
- ❑ Mocking
- ❑ Treating like a servant
- ❑ Gaslighting
    - ❑ What is gaslighting? Gaslighting is a form of emotional abuse that allows the abuser to maintain complete power and control. With this method, gaslighting causes the victim to question their sanity, memory, mental state or feelings through certain actions like:

➔ Denying previous abusive behavior ever happened

➔ Calling the victim crazy or too sensitive, or overly emotional

➔ Describing an event that happened in a completely different manner

Through these forms of control, you're more likely to stay in the relationship because you're uncertain of your own selective memory.

Statistics:

- ❑ 48.4% of women and 48.8% of men have experienced at least one psychologically aggressive behavior by an intimate partner
- ❑ 17.9% of women have experienced a situation where an intimate partner tried to keep them from seeing family and friends
- ❑ 18.7% of women have experienced threats of physical harm by an intimate partner
- ❑ 95% of men who physically abuse their intimate partners also psychologically abuse them.

Why it Matters?

- Psychological abuse increases the trauma of physical and sexual abuse, and a number of studies have demonstrated that psychological abuse independently causes long-term damage to a victim's mental health.
- Victims of psychological abuse often experience depression, post-traumatic stress disorder, suicidal ideation, low self-esteem, and difficulty trusting others. Subtle psychological abuse is more harmful than either overt psychological abuse or direct aggression

Effects of Psychological Abuse:

- 7 out of 10 psychologically abused women display symptoms of PTSD and/or depression.
- Women experiencing psychological abuse are significantly more likely to report poor physical and mental health and to have more than 5 physician visits in the last year.
- Psychological abuse is a stronger predictor of PTSD than physical abuse among women.

National Coalition Against Domestic Violence (NCADV). (2015). "Domestic Violence" Facts About Domestic Violence and Psychological Abuse. Fact Sheet. Retrieved from www.ncadv.org and pd

<u>Stalking:</u> ***According to the National Coalition Against Domestic Violence***

Stalking is defined by law by the federal government. When an abuser acts in such a way as to intentionally create a fear of harm or death for the victim, that is stalking. This could take the form of a fear of harm, injury or death for themselves, a relative, or any third party. Abusers who use stalking to terrorize and threaten create substantial emotional distress for their victims, family members and third parties. Stalking may occur through use of technology, including but not limited to, email, telephone, voicemail, text messaging, and use of GPS and social networking sites.

Statistics:

- ❑ 1 in every 6 U.S. women and 1 out of every 19 U.S. men have been stalked in their lifetime.
- ❑ Nearly 3 out of 4 victims of stalking know their stalkers in some capacity. The most common relationship between the victim and perpetrator is a current or former intimate partner
- ❑ People aged 18-24 have the highest rate of stalking victimization. Although stalking is a crime in all 50 states, less than 1/3 of states classify stalking as a felony if it is a first offense, leaving stalking victims without protections afforded to victims of other violent crimes.

Impact on Victims:

- ❑ 1 in 7 stalking victims have been forced to move.
- ❑ 1 in 8 stalking victims has reported losing work because of the stalking. More than half of these victims reported losing 5 or more work days.
- ❑ Stalking victims suffer much higher rates of depression, anxiety, insomnia, and social dysfunction than people in the general population.
- ❑ 86% of victims surveyed reported their personalities had changed as a result of being stalked.
- ❑ 37% victims of stalking fulfill all the diagnostic criteria for post-traumatic stress disorder; an additional 18% fulfilled all but one diagnostic criteria.
- ❑ 1 in 4 stalking victims contemplate suicide

National Coalition Against Domestic Violence (NCADV). (2015). "Domestic Violence" Facts about domestic violence and stalking. Fact Sheet. Retrieved from www.ncadv.org and pdf

A diagram called the "Power and Control Wheel," developed by the Domestic Abuse Intervention Project in Duluth, identifies the various behaviors that are used by batterers to gain power and control over their victims. The wheel demonstrates the relationship between physical and sexual violence and the tactics of intimidation, coercion, and manipulation that are often used by batterers.

Domestic Abuse Intervention: "Power and Control Wheel," Project in Duluth (1993)

Resources for Victims of Domestic Violence & Sexual Assault

RESOURCES

WE ARE HERE TO SUPPORT!!! YOU ARE NOT IN THIS ALONE.
IN THE EVENT OF AN EMERGENCY CALL 911.
The following agencies provide national assistance for victims of domestic and family violence:

NATIONAL ORGANIZATIONS

National Child Abuse Hotline- www.childhelp.org (1.800.422.4453)

National Domestic Violence Hotline- www.ndvh.org (1.800.799.7233)

National Teen Dating Abuse Helpline- www.loveisrespect.org (1.866.331.9474)

National Suicide Prevention Lifeline- www.suicidepreventionlifeline.org (1.800.273.8255)

Centers for Disease Control and Prevention (800-CDC-INFO)
TTY: 888-232-6348

The coalition of Labor Union Women- 202-466-4615

Corporate Alliance to End Partner Violence: 309-664-0667

Employers Against Domestic Violence: 508-894-6322

Futures without Violence: 415-678-5500/TTY 800-595-4889

National Coalition Against Domestic Violence (www.ncadv.org)

National Network to End Domestic Violence: 202-543-5566

National Resource Center on Domestic Violence: 800-537-2238

National Sexual Violence Resource Center: 717-909-0710

Rape Abuse and Incest National Network (RAINN): 800-656-HOPE

Sexual Assault Training and Investigations (SATI) (mysati.com): 619-561-3845

Speaking Out About Rape (SOAR)- 407-898-0693

Stalking Resource Center, National Center for Victims of Crime 1-800-FYI-CALL (394-2255)/TTY: 800-211-7996

The Battered Women's Justice Project: 800-903-0111

The National Center for Victims of Crime (www.victimsofcrime.org)

The National Domestic Violence Hotline (www.thehotline.org): 800-799-7233 or TTY 1-800-787-3224

U.S. Department of Justice, Office on Violence Against Women: 202-307-6026

Workplaces Respond to Domestic and Sexual Violence: A National Resource Center (www.workplacesrespond.org)

STATE COALITIONS

Alabama Coalition Against Domestic Violence
P. O. Box 4762
Montgomery, AL 36101
Hotline: 1 (800) 650-6522
Office: (334) 832-4842 Fax: (334) 832-4803
Website: www.acadv.org
Email: info@acadv.org

Alaska Network on Domestic Violence & Sexual Assault
130 Seward Street, Suite 214
Juneau, AK 99801
Office: (907) 586-3650
Website: www.andvsa.org
Email: andvsa@andvsa.org

Arizona Coalition Against Domestic Violence
2800 N. Central Ave., Suite 1570
Phoenix, AZ 85004
Hotline: 1 (800) 782-6400
Office: (602) 279-2900 Fax: (602) 279-2980
Website: www.azcadv.org
Email: info@azcadv.org

Arkansas Coalition Against Domestic Violence
1401 W. Capitol Avenue, Suite 170
Little Rock, AR 72201
Hotline: 1 (800) 269-4668
Office: (501) 907-5612 Fax: (501) 907-5618
Website: www.domesticpeace.com

California Partnership to End Domestic Violence
P. O. Box 1798
Sacramento, CA 95812
Office: (916) 444-7163 Fax: (916) 444-7165
Website: www.cpedv.org
Email: info@cpedv.org

Colorado Coalition Against Domestic Violence
1120 Lincoln St, #900
Denver, CO 80203
Office: (303) 831-9632
Website: www.ccadv.org

Connecticut Coalition Against Domestic Violence
912 Silas Deane Highway, Lower Level
Wethersfield, CT 06109
Hotline: (888) 774-2900
Office: (860) 282-7899 Fax: (860) 282-7892
Website: www.ctcadv.org

Delaware Coalition Against Domestic Violence
100 W. 10th Street, Suite 903
Wilmington, DE 19801
Northern Delaware: (302) 762-6110
Southern Delaware: (302) 422-8058 Bilingual: (302) 745-9874
Office: (302) 658-2958- Website: www.dcadv.org

DC Coalition Against Domestic Violence
5 Thomas Circle, NW
Washington, DC 20005
Office: (202) 299-1181 Fax: (202) 299-1193
Website: www.dccadv.org
Email: info@dccadv.org

Florida Coalition Against Domestic Violence
425 Office Plaza
Tallahassee, FL 32301
Hotline: (800) 500-1119
TDD: (850) 621-4202
Office: (850) 425-2749 Fax: (850) 425-3091
Website: www.fcadv.org

Georgia Coalition Against Domestic Violence
114 New Street, Suite B
Decatur, GA 30030
Hotline: 1 (800) 334-2836
Office: (404) 209-0280 Fax: (404) 766-3800
Website: www.gcadv.org

Hawaii State Coalition Against Domestic Violence
810 Richards Street, Suite 960
Honolulu, HI 96813
Office: (808) 832-9316 Fax: (808) 841-6028
Website: www.hscadv.org

Idaho Coalition Against Sexual & Domestic Violence
300 E. Mallard Drive, Suite 130
Boise, ID 83706
Office: (208) 384-0419
Website: www.idvsa.org
Email: info@engagingvoices.org

Illinois Coalition Against Domestic Violence
Hotline: (877) 863-6338
Office: (217) 789-2830
Website: www.ilcadv.org

Indiana Coalition Against Domestic Violence
1915 W. 18th Street, Suite B
Indianapolis, IN 46202
Hotline: 1 (800) 332-7385
Office: (317) 917-3685 Fax: (317) 917-3695
Website: www.icadvinc.org

Iowa Coalition against Domestic Violence
3030 Merle Hay Road
Des Moines, IA 50310
Hotline: 1 (800) 942-0333
Office: (515) 244-8028 Fax: (515) 244-7417
Website: www.icadv.org
Email: icadv@icadv.org

Kansas Coalition against Sexual & Domestic Violence
634 SW Harrison Street
Topeka, KS 66603
Hotline: 1 (888) 363-2287
Office: (785) 232-9784 Fax: (785) 266-1874
Website: www.kcsdv.org

Kentucky Domestic Violence Association
111 Darby Shire Circle
Frankfort, KY 40601
Office: (502) 209-5382 Fax: (502) 226-5382
Website: www.kdva.org
Email: info@kdva.org

Louisiana Coalition Against Domestic Violence
P.O. Box 77308
Baton Rouge, LA 70879
Hotline: 1 (888) 411-1333
Office: (225) 752-1296
Website: www.lcadv.org

Maine Coalition to End Domestic Violence
One Weston Court, Box#2
Augusta, ME 04330
Hotline: 1 (866) 834-4357
Office: (207) 430-8334 Fax: (207) 430-8348
Website: www.mcedv.org
Email: info@mcedv.org

Maryland Network Against Domestic Violence
4601 Presidents Dr., Ste. 370
Lanham, MD 20706
Hotline: 1 (800) 634-3577
Office: (301) 429-3601 Fax: (301) 429-3605
Website: www.mnadv.org
Email: info@mnadv.org

Massachusetts Coalition Against Sexual Assault & Domestic Violence/Jane Doe, Inc.
14 Beacon Street, Suite 507
Boston, MA 02108
Hotline: 1 (877) 785-2020
TTY/TTD: 1 (877) 521-2601
Office: (617) 248-0922 Fax: (617) 248-0902
Website: www.janedoe.org
Email: info@janedoe.org

Michigan Coalition To End Domestic & Sexual Violence
3893 Okemos Road, Suite B2
Okemos, MI 48864
Office: (517) 347-7000 Fax: (517) 347-1377
TTY: (517) 381-8470
Website: www.mcedsv.org

Minnesota Coalition for Battered Women
60 Plato Blvd. E, Suite 130
Saint Paul, MN 55107
Hotline: 1 (866) 223-1111
Office: (651) 646-6177 Fax: (651) 646-1527
Website: www.mcbw.org

Mississippi Coalition Against Domestic Violence
P.O. Box 4703
Jackson, MS 39296
Hotline: 1 (800) 898-3234
Office: (601) 981-9196 Fax: (601) 981-2501
Website: www.mcadv.org
Email: support@mcadv.org

Missouri Coalition Against Domestic & Sexual Violence
217 Oscar Dr., Suite A
Jefferson City, MO 65101
Office: (573) 634-4161
Website: www.mocadsv.org

Montana Coalition Against Domestic & Sexual Violence
32 S Ewing St
Helena, MT 59601
Office: (406) 443-7794
Website: www.mcadsv.com
Email: mtcoalition@mcadsv.com

Nebraska Domestic Violence Sexual Assault Coalition
245 South 84th St, Suite 200
Lincoln, NE 68510
Office: (402) 476-6256 Fax: (402) 476-6806
Spanish Hotline: (877) 215-0167
Website: www.ndvsac.org

Nevada Network Against Domestic Violence
250 South Rock Bldvd., Suite 116
Reno, NV 89502
(775) 828-1115 Fax: (775) 828-9911
Website: www.nnadv.org

New Hampshire Coalition Against Domestic & Sexual Violence
P.O. Box 353
Concord, NH 03302
Hotline: 1 (866) 644-3574
Office: (603) 224-8893 Fax: (603) 228-6096
Website: www.nhcadsv.org

New Jersey Coalition for Battered Women
1670 Whitehorse Hamilton Square
Trenton, NJ 08690
Hotline: 1 (800) 572-7233 TTY: (800) 787-3224
Office: (609) 584-8107 Fax: (609) 584-9750
Website: www.njcbw.org

New Mexico Coalition Against Domestic Violence
1210 Luisa Street, Suite 7
Santa Fe, NM 87505
Office: (505) 246-9240 Fax: (505) 246-9240
Website: www.nmcadv.org
Email: info@nmcadv.org

New York State Coalition Against Domestic Violence
119 Washington Avenue, 3rd Floor
Albany, NY 12210
Hotline NYS: 1 (800) 942-6906
Hotline NYC: 1 (800) 621-4673
Office: (518) 482-5465 Fax: (518) 482-3807
Website: www.nyscadv.org

North Carolina Coalition Against Domestic Violence
3710 University Drive, Suite 140
Durham, NC 27707
Office: (919) 956-9124 Fax: (919) 682-1449
Website: www.nccadv.org

North Dakota Council on Abused Women's Services
525 N. 4th St.
Bismark, ND 58501
Office: (701) 255-6240 Fax: (701) 255-1904
Website: www.ndcaws.org
Ohio Domestic Violence Network
Hotline: (800) 934-9840
Website: www.odvn.org

Oklahoma Coalition Against Domestic Violence & Sexual Assault
3815 N. Santa Fe Ave., Suite 124
Oklahoma City, OK 73118
Hotline: 1 (800) 522-7233
Office: (405) 524-0700 TTY: (405) 512-5577
Website: www.ocadvsa.org
Email: info@ocadvsa.org

Oregon Coalition Against Domestic & Sexual Violence
9570 SW Barbur Blvd., Suite 214
Portland, OR 97219
Hotline: 1 (888) 235-5333
Office: (503) 230-1951 Fax: (503) 230-1973
Website: www.ocadsv.org

Pennsylvania Coalition Against Domestic Violence
3605 Vartan Way, Suite 101
Harrisburg PA 17110
Office (717) 545-6400 TTY (800) 553-2508
Website: www.pcadv.org

Rhode Island Coalition Against Domestic Violence
422 Post Road, Suite 201
Warwick, RI 02888
Hotline: 1 (800) 494-8100
Office: (401) 467-9940 Fax: (401) 467-9943
Website: www.ricadv.org
Email: ricadv@ricadv.org

South Carolina Coalition Against Domestic Violence & Sexual Assault
P.O. Box 7776
Columbia, SC 29202
Office: (803) 256-2900
Website: www.sccadvasa.org

South Dakota Coalition Ending Domestic Violence & Sexual Assault
P.O. Box 141
Pierre, SD 57501
Office: (605) 945-0869
Website: www.sdcedsv.org

Tennessee Coalition To End Domestic & Sexual Violence
2 International Plaza Dr. Suite 425
Nashville, TN 37217
Hotline: 1 (800) 356-6767
Office: (615) 386-9406
Website: tncoalition.org

Texas Council on Family Violence
P.O. Box 163865
Austin, TX 78716
Office: (512) 794-1133 Fax: (512) 685.6397
Website: www.tcfv.org

Utah Domestic Violence Coalition
205 North 400 West,
Salt Lake City, UT 84103
Hotline: 1 (800) 897-5465
Office: (801) 521-5544
Website: www.udvc.org

Vermont Network Against Domestic & Sexual Violence
P.O. Box 405
Montpelier, VT 05601
Hotline: 1 (800) 228-7395
Office: (802) 223-1302 Fax: (802) 223-6943
Website: www.vtnetwork.org
Email: vtnetwork@vtnetwork.org

Virginia Sexual & Domestic Violence Action Alliance
5008 Monument Avenue, Suite A
Richmond, VA 23230
Office: (804) 377-0335
Website: www.vsdvalliance.org
Email: info@vsdvalliance.org

Washington State Coalition Against Domestic Violence
711 Capitol Way, Suite 702
Olympia, WA 98501
Hotline: 1 (800) 562-6025
Office: (360) 586-1022 Fax: (360) 586-1024
Website: www.wscadv.org
Email: wscadv@wscadv.org

West Virginia Coalition Against Domestic Violence
5004 Elk River Road, South
Elkview, WV 25071
Office: (304) 965-3552 Fax: (304) 965-3572
Website: www.wvcadv.org

Wisconsin Coalition Against Domestic Violence
1245 E. Washington Ave, Suite 150
Madison, WI 53703
Office: (608) 255-0539 Fax: (608) 255-3560
Website: endabusewi.org
Email: wcadv@wcadv.org

Wyoming Coalition Against Domestic Violence & Sexual Assault
P.O. Box 236
710 Garfield Street, Suite 218
Laramie, WY 82073
Office: (307) 755-5481 Fax: (307) 755-5482
Website: www.wyomingdvsa.org

Creating A Safety Plan

Adopted by ©Peel Committee Against Woman Abuse. "Safety Plan" Second edition: March 2004. Third edition: July 2005. Fourth edition: April 2006. Fifth edition: July 2010.

I. INTRODUCTION

The time of separation from an abusive person is or can be the most dangerous time of the relationship This is because it is when the abuser's power and control over the relationship is the most threatened

This plan was designed to provide women with strategies to increase their safety. Whether you are living in an abusive relationship, thinking about leaving an abusive relationship, or have already left an abusive relationship, there are a number of ways in which you can increase your safety and that of your children.

Whenever the potential for violence is identified in a woman's life, it is important to develop a safety plan. Creating a safety plan involves identifying action steps to increase safety, and to prepare in advance for the possibility of further violence.

Since abusive situations and risk factors can change quickly, it is recommended that you become familiar with, and review and/or revise your safety plan regularly.

In creating a safety plan, it is important to remember that:

- ❑ You are not to blame for thc abuse or for your children's exposure to it
- ❑ You are not responsible for your (ex) partner's abusive behavior
- ❑ You cannot control your (ex) partner's violence, but it may be possible to increase your own safety as well as the safety of your children
- ❑ The safety of you and your children is always the most important thing
- ❑ You are not alone. There are community resources available to provide support in a number of ways (counselling, housing, financial assistance, etc.)

II. TAKING CARE OF YOURSELF One of the most crucial, yet frequently overlooked, aspects of safety and safety planning is taking care of yourself. This includes your physical, emotional and spiritual wellbeing. It is important to understand some of what you, as a woman who has experienced abuse, may be dealing with. You may be:

- ❑ experiencing ongoing abuse, threats of abuse, or surviving the impacts and trauma of past abuse
- ❑ fearful for your safety and your children's safety
- ❑ dealing with practical problems such as finding housing, financial support, and/or employment
- ❑ feeling isolated, alone, overwhelmed, helpless and/or hopeless
- ❑ feeling blamed for the abuse and/ or your children's exposure to it
- ❑ fearful of being an outcast in your family or community
- ❑ fearful of losing your children because of their exposure to the abuse
- ❑ accused of being an unfit mother

Trying to survive in or escape an abusive relationship can be exhausting and emotionally draining. There are a number of things you can do to help you cope in difficult times. These are just a few suggestions:

- ❑ Always remember that safety – your own as well as the safety of your children – is what matters the most
- ❑ If you have left the relationship, are feeling down and are considering returning to a potentially abusive situation, call a friend, relative, counsellor, etc. for support
- ❑ Get connected to community resources. There are lots of organizations that can help make your journey a little easier and can assist in navigating the way to services and supports that will meet your needs
- ❑ When you have to communicate with your ex/partner, in person or by telephone, arrange to have a trusted and supportive friend/relative present
- ❑ Attend as many counselling sessions as you can and become involved in community activities to reduce feeling isolated

- ❑ Take time for yourself (read, meditate, play music, etc.)
- ❑ Fulfill your spiritual needs in whatever way is appropriate for you
- ❑ Write or talk about your feelings, especially when you are feeling low or vulnerable
- ❑ Take time to prepare yourself emotionally before entering stressful situations like talking with your partner, meeting with lawyers, or attending court, etc.
- ❑ Try not to overbook yourself - limit yourself to one appointment per day to reduce stress. Write down the dates, times, and locations of your appointments

III. AN EMERGENCY ESCAPE PLAN

The Emergency Escape Plan focuses on the things you can do in advance to be better prepared in case you have to leave an abusive situation very quickly. The following is a list of items you should try to set aside and hide in a safe place (e.g. at a friend or family member's home, with your lawyer, in a safety deposit box):

A) Make a photocopy of the following items and store in a safe place, away from the originals. Hide the originals someplace else, if you can.

- ❑ Passports, birth certificates, Indian/First Nations status cards, citizenship papers, immigration papers, permanent resident or citizenship cards, etc. for all family members
- ❑ Driver's license, registration, insurance papers
- ❑ Prescriptions, medical & vaccination records for family members
- ❑ School records
- ❑ Marriage certificate, divorce papers, custody documentation, court orders, restraining orders, or other legal documents
- ❑ Picture of spouse/partner
- ❑ Health cards for yourself and family members
- ❑ Lease/rental agreement, house deed, mortgage payment books.

B) Try to keep all the cards you normally use in your wallet:

- ❏ Social Insurance Number (SIN) card
- ❏ Credit cards
- ❏ Phone card
- ❏ Bank cards
- ❏ Health cards

C) Try to keep your wallet and purse handy, and containing the following:

- ❏ Keys for your home, car, workplace, safety deposit box, etc.
- ❏ Cheque book, bank books/statements
- ❏ Driver's license, registration, insurance
- ❏ Address/telephone book
- ❏ Picture of spouse/partner
- ❏ Emergency money (in cash) hidden away
- ❏ Cell phone

D) Keep the following items handy, so you can grab them quickly:

- ❏ Emergency suitcase containing immediate needs or a suitcase that you can pack quickly
- ❏ Special toys and/or comforts for your children
- ❏ Medications
- ❏ Jewelry and small saleable objects
- ❏ Items of special sentimental value
- ❏ A list of other items you would like to take if you get a chance to return to your home to collect more belongings late

E) Other Considerations:

- ❑ Open a bank account in your own name and arrange that no bank statements or other calls be made to you. Or, arrange that mail be sent to a trusted friend or family member.
- ❑ Save and set aside as much money as you can (e.g. a bit of change out of grocery-money if/when possible).
- ❑ Locate your local food bank so you can save money on groceries.
- ❑ Hide extra clothing, keys, money, etc. at a friend/family member's house.
- ❑ Plan your emergency exits, taking into consideration mobility and accessibility concerns, as well as appropriate modes of transportation and how to arrange it (e.g. taxi, bus, TransHelp, Wheel-Trans, etc.).
- ❑ Keep an emergency suitcase packed or handy/ready to pack quickly.

IV. CREATING A SAFER ENVIRONMENT There are many things a woman can do to increase her safety. It may not be possible to do everything at once, but safety measures can be added step-by-step over time. Here are a few suggestions:

A) AT HOME If you are living with your abusive partner:

- ❑ Get your Emergency Escape Plan in order and review it often.
- ❑ Create a list of telephone numbers including local police, nearest women's shelter, Assaulted Women's Help Line, family members, friends, counsellors, children's friends, etc.
- ❑ Make arrangements with friends or family so that you can stay with them if necessary.
- ❑ Notice what triggers your partner's violence and abuse. This can help you try to predict the next likely incident and give you a chance to prepare (i.e. by making plans for the children to be sent to friends/family in advance).

- ❑ If you have call display on your phone, be careful about who can get access to stored numbers such as the last number you dialed or received a call from.
- ❑ Check your vehicle for a Global Positioning System (GPS) which your abuser may have installed in or under your car to track your movements. Teach your children to use the telephone (and cell phone, if you have one) to contact the police and the fire department.
- ❑ Teach your children how to make a collect call to you and to a special friend if your partner takes the children.
- ❑ Create a code word with your children and/or family/ friends so they know when to call for help.
- ❑ Plan your emergency exits and teach them to your children.
- ❑ Teach your children their own Safety Plan
- ❑ Consider a plan for the safety and wellbeing of your pet(s) such as making arrangements with friends or family to care for them if need be.
- ❑ Be aware of any weapons in the home or your partner's access to weapons

If you are not living with your abusive partner:

- ❑ Instruct those who know of your whereabouts to tell your abusive partner, if asked, that they do not know where you are or how to contact you.
- ❑ Change the locks on the doors, windows, garage and mailbox.
- ❑ Install a peephole in the door that your children can see through as well. If possible, install an alarm system.
- ❑ Keep doors and windows locked at all times.
- ❑ Have a pre-recorded anonymous message on your telephone answering service rather than your own voice and do not identify yourself by name.
- ❑ If possible, trade in your car for a different make and model.
- ❑ Consider the advantages of getting a dog that barks when someone approaches your house, or get a "Beware of Dog" sign.

- ❑ Install a lighting system outside your home that lights up when a person is coming close to your house.
- ❑ Do whatever you can to increase security, including additional locks, window bars, poles to wedge against doors, an electronic system, etc., and keep trees and bushes trimmed – anything to provide added security.
- ❑ Electronic security measures when using the computer may also be helpful including changing your passwords, creating new email addresses for yourself and your children, blocking unwanted emails and/or senders, etc.
- ❑ If you agree to see your partner, meet in a public place and limit your isolation. Make sure someone knows where you are and when to expect you to return.
- ❑ If your abusive partner has legal access to your children, talk to a lawyer about getting supervised access or having access denied.

B) IN THE NEIGHBORHOOD

- ❑ Tell your neighbors that you would like them to call the police if they hear a fight or screaming in your home.
- ❑ Tell people who take care of your children, including schools and daycares, which people have permission to pick up your children.
- ❑ Tell the school, daycare, babysitter, and people who have permission to pick up your children that your (ex) partner is not permitted to do so and ask that they not give your contact information to anyone.
- ❑ Tell people in your neighborhood that your partner no longer lives with you, and they should call the police if he/she is seen near your home. You may wish to give them a photo and description of him/her and of his/her car.
- ❑ Ask your neighbors to look after your children in an emergency.

C) AT WORK Each woman must decide for herself if and/or when she will tell others that her partner is abusive and that she may be at risk. Friends, family and co-workers may be able to help protect you. However, each woman should consider carefully which people to ask for help. If you are comfortable, you may choose to do any or all of the following:

- ❏ Show a picture of your ex/partner and provide a description of his/ her car to colleagues, neighbors, and building security personnel to make them aware and alert to your safety needs.
- ❏ Tell your boss, the security supervisor, and other key people or friends at work about your situation, and ask that they refrain from giving anyone personal information about you.
- ❏ Ask to have your calls screened at work or use voicemail to screen your calls. Document any unwanted calls from your abuser.
- ❏ Discuss the possibility of having your employer call the police if you are in danger from your ex/partner.
- ❏ Block unwanted emails or send them to a folder where you do not have to read them.

V. A CHILD'S SAFETY PLAN This plan was developed to help mothers teach their children some basic safety planning.

It is based on the belief that the most important thing that children can do for their mothers and their families is to get away from the area of violence. Although children often try to stop the violence by distracting the abuser or directly interfering in the abusive episode. It is important to tell children that the best and most important thing for them to do is to keep themselves safe.

Children who are exposed to woman abuse can be profoundly affected. It is very traumatic for them to be faced with violence directed at them or at someone they love. Personal safety and safety planning are extremely important and necessary for children whose families are experiencing violence. Children should learn ways to protect themselves. Tell your children that their only job is to keep themselves safe. There are several ways to help you develop a safety plan with your children:

- ❏ Have your child pick a safe room/place in the house, preferably with a lock on the door and a phone. The first step of any plan is for the children to get out of the room where the abuse is occurring.
- ❏ Stress the importance of being safe, and that it is not the child's responsibility to make sure that his/her mother is safe.
- ❏ Create a code word to use with your children so that they know when to run to safety and to call for help.
- ❏ Teach your children how to call for help. It is important that children know they should not use a phone that is in view of the abuser. This puts them at risk. Talk to your children 18 about using a neighbor's phone or a pay phone if they are unable to use a phone at home. Remember that there is no cost when dialing 911 from a pay phone or cell phone.
- ❏ If you have a cell phone, teach your children how to use it. Teach them how to contact the police by dialing 911.
- ❏ Ensure that the children know their full name and address (rural children need to know their Concession and Lot #). Rehearse what your child/children will say when they call for help
- ❏ It is important for children to leave the phone off the hook after they are done talking. The police may call the number back if they hang up, which could create a dangerous situation for yourself and your children.
- ❏ Pick a safe place to meet your children, out of the home, so you can easily find each other after the situation is safe.
- ❏ Teach your children the safest route for them to take to the planned place of safety.

Practice and role-play this safety-plan with your children including what to do and where to go if something scary or violent happens.

1. NCADV. (2015). Facts About Domestic Violence and Physical Abuse. Retrieved from www.ncadv.org

2. NCADV. (2015). Facts About Domestic Violence and Psychological Abuse. Retrieved from www.ncadv.org

3. NCADV. (2015). Facts About Domestic Violence and Economic Abuse. Retrieved from www.ncadv.org

4. NCADV. (2015). Facts About Domestic Violence and Stalking. Retrieved from www.ncadv.org

5. National Coalition Against Domestic Violence (2017). Domestic violence and sexual assault. Retrieved from www.ncadv.org

6. http://ncadv.org/files/Domestic%20Violence%20and%20Sexual%20Abuse%20NCADV.pdf.

7. National center on elder abuse. Washington DC: 2005. Fact Sheet: Domestic violence: Older women can be victims too. [Google Scholar]

8. Peel Committee Against Woman Abuse. Second edition: March 2004. Third edition: July 2005. Fourth edition: April 2006. Fifth edition: July 2010.

9. The Duluth Model-Power and Control Wheel (Domestic Abuse Intervention Project, n.d. circa 1993)

10. Zimmerman C. Plates in a basket will rattle: Domestic violence in Combodia, Phnom Pehn. Combodia: The Asia Foundation; 1994

Thank You For

Your Support!

Made in the USA
Columbia, SC
24 August 2019